Adventurous RV

ADVENTUROUS RV

The Ultimate Logbook for those
Charting their Own Course

David A. Ogren

Adventurous RV: The Ultimate Logbook for those Charting their Own Course.

Copyright © 2019: David A. Ogren

All rights reserved.

No part of this book may be reproduced or transmitted in any form or by any means whatsoever without express written permission from the author, except in the case of brief quotations embodied in critical articles and reviews.

Additional Publications by David A. Ogren

The Last Bucket List: Think Big. Be Changed. Give Life

Acoustic Guitar Care 101: A Survival Guide for Beginners

GuitarQuotes: Inspiration from the World's Best Players

Market to Millions: The Ultimate Directory to Free eBook Promotion

RV PARK/CAMPGROUND: _____
DATE(S) VISITED: _____
SITE NUMBER: _____
OVERALL RATING ☆ ☆ ☆ ☆ ☆

BASIC CAMPSITE INFORMATION

- [ ] PULL-THROUGH
- [ ] BACK-IN
- [ ] SECLUDED SITE
- [ ] 50 AMP
- [ ] 30 AMP
- [ ] OPEN SITE
- [ ] WATER
- [ ] SEWER
- [ ] CONCRETE PAD

ADDITIONAL AMENITIES

- [ ] LAUNDRY
- [ ] WI-FI
- [ ] GAME RENTALS
- [ ] FIRE RING
- [ ] CABLE TV
- [ ] HIKING TRAILS
- [ ] SPORT ACTIVITY
- [ ] FITNESS ROOM
- [ ] FISHING
- [ ] POOL
- [ ] CLUBHOUSE
- [ ] BOATING
- [ ] RECEIVES MAIL
- [ ] SHOWERS
- [ ] ON-SITE STORE

NOISE LEVEL
- [ ] ACCEPTABLE
- [ ] UNACCEPTABLE

EXTRA FEES
- [ ] KIDS
- [ ] PETS

CLEANLINESS
- [ ] ACCEPTABLE
- [ ] UNACCEPTABLE

Surprising things we saw

Special events/outings

New acquaintances made

Miscellaneous notes

RV PARK/CAMPGROUND: _____

DATE(S) VISITED: _____

SITE NUMBER: _____

OVERALL RATING ☆ ☆ ☆ ☆ ☆

BASIC CAMPSITE INFORMATION

- ☐ PULL-THROUGH
- ☐ BACK-IN
- ☐ SECLUDED SITE
- ☐ 50 AMP
- ☐ 30 AMP
- ☐ OPEN SITE
- ☐ WATER
- ☐ SEWER
- ☐ CONCRETE PAD

ADDITIONAL AMENITIES

- ☐ LAUNDRY
- ☐ WI-FI
- ☐ GAME RENTALS
- ☐ FIRE RING
- ☐ CABLE TV
- ☐ HIKING TRAILS
- ☐ SPORT ACTIVITY
- ☐ FITNESS ROOM
- ☐ FISHING
- ☐ POOL
- ☐ CLUBHOUSE
- ☐ BOATING
- ☐ RECEIVES MAIL
- ☐ SHOWERS
- ☐ ON-SITE STORE

NOISE LEVEL
- ☐ ACCEPTABLE
- ☐ UNACCEPTABLE

EXTRA FEES
- ☐ KIDS
- ☐ PETS

CLEANLINESS
- ☐ ACCEPTABLE
- ☐ UNACCEPTABLE

Surprising things we saw

Special events/outings

New acquaintances made

Miscellaneous notes

RV PARK/CAMPGROUND: _____

DATE(S) VISITED: _____

SITE NUMBER: _____

OVERALL RATING ☆ ☆ ☆ ☆ ☆

BASIC CAMPSITE INFORMATION

- [ ] PULL-THROUGH
- [ ] BACK-IN
- [ ] SECLUDED SITE
- [ ] 50 AMP
- [ ] 30 AMP
- [ ] OPEN SITE
- [ ] WATER
- [ ] SEWER
- [ ] CONCRETE PAD

ADDITIONAL AMENITIES

- [ ] LAUNDRY
- [ ] WI-FI
- [ ] GAME RENTALS
- [ ] FIRE RING
- [ ] CABLE TV
- [ ] HIKING TRAILS
- [ ] SPORT ACTIVITY
- [ ] FITNESS ROOM
- [ ] FISHING
- [ ] POOL
- [ ] CLUBHOUSE
- [ ] BOATING
- [ ] RECEIVES MAIL
- [ ] SHOWERS
- [ ] ON-SITE STORE

NOISE LEVEL
- [ ] ACCEPTABLE
- [ ] UNACCEPTABLE

EXTRA FEES
- [ ] KIDS
- [ ] PETS

CLEANLINESS
- [ ] ACCEPTABLE
- [ ] UNACCEPTABLE

Surprising things we saw

_____
_____
_____
_____
_____
_____
_____
_____
_____
_____

Special events/outings

_____
_____
_____
_____
_____
_____
_____
_____
_____
_____

New acquaintances made

_____
_____
_____
_____
_____
_____
_____
_____
_____
_____

Miscellaneous notes

_____
_____
_____
_____
_____
_____
_____
_____
_____
_____

RV PARK/CAMPGROUND: _____

DATE(S) VISITED: _____

SITE NUMBER: _____

OVERALL RATING ☆☆☆☆☆

BASIC CAMPSITE INFORMATION

- [ ] PULL-THROUGH
- [ ] BACK-IN
- [ ] SECLUDED SITE
- [ ] 50 AMP
- [ ] 30 AMP
- [ ] OPEN SITE
- [ ] WATER
- [ ] SEWER
- [ ] CONCRETE PAD

ADDITIONAL AMENITIES

- [ ] LAUNDRY
- [ ] WI-FI
- [ ] GAME RENTALS
- [ ] FIRE RING
- [ ] CABLE TV
- [ ] HIKING TRAILS
- [ ] SPORT ACTIVITY
- [ ] FITNESS ROOM
- [ ] FISHING
- [ ] POOL
- [ ] CLUBHOUSE
- [ ] BOATING
- [ ] RECEIVES MAIL
- [ ] SHOWERS
- [ ] ON-SITE STORE

NOISE LEVEL
- [ ] ACCEPTABLE
- [ ] UNACCEPTABLE

EXTRA FEES
- [ ] KIDS
- [ ] PETS

CLEANLINESS
- [ ] ACCEPTABLE
- [ ] UNACCEPTABLE

Surprising things we saw

Special events/outings

New acquaintances made

Miscellaneous notes

RV PARK/CAMPGROUND: _____

DATE(S) VISITED: _____

SITE NUMBER: _____

OVERALL RATING ☆ ☆ ☆ ☆ ☆

BASIC CAMPSITE INFORMATION

- [ ] PULL-THROUGH
- [ ] BACK-IN
- [ ] SECLUDED SITE
- [ ] 50 AMP
- [ ] 30 AMP
- [ ] OPEN SITE
- [ ] WATER
- [ ] SEWER
- [ ] CONCRETE PAD

ADDITIONAL AMENITIES

- [ ] LAUNDRY
- [ ] WI-FI
- [ ] GAME RENTALS
- [ ] FIRE RING
- [ ] CABLE TV
- [ ] HIKING TRAILS
- [ ] SPORT ACTIVITY
- [ ] FITNESS ROOM
- [ ] FISHING
- [ ] POOL
- [ ] CLUBHOUSE
- [ ] BOATING
- [ ] RECEIVES MAIL
- [ ] SHOWERS
- [ ] ON-SITE STORE

NOISE LEVEL
- [ ] ACCEPTABLE
- [ ] UNACCEPTABLE

EXTRA FEES
- [ ] KIDS
- [ ] PETS

CLEANLINESS
- [ ] ACCEPTABLE
- [ ] UNACCEPTABLE

Surprising things we saw

Special events/outings

New acquaintances made

Miscellaneous notes

RV PARK/CAMPGROUND: _____
DATE(S) VISITED: _____
SITE NUMBER: _____
OVERALL RATING ☆☆☆☆☆

BASIC CAMPSITE INFORMATION

- [ ] PULL-THROUGH
- [ ] BACK-IN
- [ ] SECLUDED SITE
- [ ] 50 AMP
- [ ] 30 AMP
- [ ] OPEN SITE
- [ ] WATER
- [ ] SEWER
- [ ] CONCRETE PAD

ADDITIONAL AMENITIES

- [ ] LAUNDRY
- [ ] WI-FI
- [ ] GAME RENTALS
- [ ] FIRE RING
- [ ] CABLE TV
- [ ] HIKING TRAILS
- [ ] SPORT ACTIVITY
- [ ] FITNESS ROOM
- [ ] FISHING
- [ ] POOL
- [ ] CLUBHOUSE
- [ ] BOATING
- [ ] RECEIVES MAIL
- [ ] SHOWERS
- [ ] ON-SITE STORE

NOISE LEVEL
- [ ] ACCEPTABLE
- [ ] UNACCEPTABLE

EXTRA FEES
- [ ] KIDS
- [ ] PETS

CLEANLINESS
- [ ] ACCEPTABLE
- [ ] UNACCEPTABLE

Surprising things we saw

Special events/outings

New acquaintances made

Miscellaneous notes

RV PARK/CAMPGROUND: _____

DATE(S) VISITED: _____

SITE NUMBER: _____

OVERALL RATING ☆ ☆ ☆ ☆ ☆

BASIC CAMPSITE INFORMATION

- [ ] PULL-THROUGH
- [ ] BACK-IN
- [ ] SECLUDED SITE
- [ ] 50 AMP
- [ ] 30 AMP
- [ ] OPEN SITE
- [ ] WATER
- [ ] SEWER
- [ ] CONCRETE PAD

ADDITIONAL AMENITIES

- [ ] LAUNDRY
- [ ] WI-FI
- [ ] GAME RENTALS
- [ ] FIRE RING
- [ ] CABLE TV
- [ ] HIKING TRAILS
- [ ] SPORT ACTIVITY
- [ ] FITNESS ROOM
- [ ] FISHING
- [ ] POOL
- [ ] CLUBHOUSE
- [ ] BOATING
- [ ] RECEIVES MAIL
- [ ] SHOWERS
- [ ] ON-SITE STORE

NOISE LEVEL
- [ ] ACCEPTABLE
- [ ] UNACCEPTABLE

EXTRA FEES
- [ ] KIDS
- [ ] PETS

CLEANLINESS
- [ ] ACCEPTABLE
- [ ] UNACCEPTABLE

Surprising things we saw

Special events/outings

New acquaintances made

Miscellaneous notes

RV PARK/CAMPGROUND: _____

DATE(S) VISITED: _____

SITE NUMBER: _____

OVERALL RATING ☆ ☆ ☆ ☆ ☆

BASIC CAMPSITE INFORMATION

- [ ] PULL-THROUGH
- [ ] BACK-IN
- [ ] SECLUDED SITE
- [ ] 50 AMP
- [ ] 30 AMP
- [ ] OPEN SITE
- [ ] WATER
- [ ] SEWER
- [ ] CONCRETE PAD

ADDITIONAL AMENITIES

- [ ] LAUNDRY
- [ ] WI-FI
- [ ] GAME RENTALS
- [ ] FIRE RING
- [ ] CABLE TV
- [ ] HIKING TRAILS
- [ ] SPORT ACTIVITY
- [ ] FITNESS ROOM
- [ ] FISHING
- [ ] POOL
- [ ] CLUBHOUSE
- [ ] BOATING
- [ ] RECEIVES MAIL
- [ ] SHOWERS
- [ ] ON-SITE STORE

NOISE LEVEL
- [ ] ACCEPTABLE
- [ ] UNACCEPTABLE

EXTRA FEES
- [ ] KIDS
- [ ] PETS

CLEANLINESS
- [ ] ACCEPTABLE
- [ ] UNACCEPTABLE

Surprising things we saw

Special events/outings

New acquaintances made

Miscellaneous notes

RV PARK/CAMPGROUND: _____

DATE(S) VISITED: _____

SITE NUMBER: _____

OVERALL RATING ☆☆☆☆☆

BASIC CAMPSITE INFORMATION

- [ ] PULL-THROUGH
- [ ] BACK-IN
- [ ] SECLUDED SITE
- [ ] 50 AMP
- [ ] 30 AMP
- [ ] OPEN SITE
- [ ] WATER
- [ ] SEWER
- [ ] CONCRETE PAD

ADDITIONAL AMENITIES

- [ ] LAUNDRY
- [ ] WI-FI
- [ ] GAME RENTALS
- [ ] FIRE RING
- [ ] CABLE TV
- [ ] HIKING TRAILS
- [ ] SPORT ACTIVITY
- [ ] FITNESS ROOM
- [ ] FISHING
- [ ] POOL
- [ ] CLUBHOUSE
- [ ] BOATING
- [ ] RECEIVES MAIL
- [ ] SHOWERS
- [ ] ON-SITE STORE

NOISE LEVEL

- [ ] ACCEPTABLE
- [ ] UNACCEPTABLE

EXTRA FEES

- [ ] KIDS
- [ ] PETS

CLEANLINESS

- [ ] ACCEPTABLE
- [ ] UNACCEPTABLE

Surprising things we saw

Special events/outings

New acquaintances made

Miscellaneous notes

RV PARK/CAMPGROUND: _____
DATE(S) VISITED: _____
SITE NUMBER: _____
OVERALL RATING ☆☆☆☆☆

BASIC CAMPSITE INFORMATION

- [ ] PULL-THROUGH
- [ ] BACK-IN
- [ ] SECLUDED SITE
- [ ] 50 AMP
- [ ] 30 AMP
- [ ] OPEN SITE
- [ ] WATER
- [ ] SEWER
- [ ] CONCRETE PAD

ADDITIONAL AMENITIES

- [ ] LAUNDRY
- [ ] WI-FI
- [ ] GAME RENTALS
- [ ] FIRE RING
- [ ] CABLE TV
- [ ] HIKING TRAILS
- [ ] SPORT ACTIVITY
- [ ] FITNESS ROOM
- [ ] FISHING
- [ ] POOL
- [ ] CLUBHOUSE
- [ ] BOATING
- [ ] RECEIVES MAIL
- [ ] SHOWERS
- [ ] ON-SITE STORE

NOISE LEVEL
- [ ] ACCEPTABLE
- [ ] UNACCEPTABLE

EXTRA FEES
- [ ] KIDS
- [ ] PETS

CLEANLINESS
- [ ] ACCEPTABLE
- [ ] UNACCEPTABLE

Surprising things we saw

Special events/outings

New acquaintances made

Miscellaneous notes

RV PARK/CAMPGROUND: _____

DATE(S) VISITED: _____

SITE NUMBER: _____

OVERALL RATING ☆ ☆ ☆ ☆ ☆

BASIC CAMPSITE INFORMATION

- [ ] PULL-THROUGH
- [ ] BACK-IN
- [ ] SECLUDED SITE
- [ ] 50 AMP
- [ ] 30 AMP
- [ ] OPEN SITE
- [ ] WATER
- [ ] SEWER
- [ ] CONCRETE PAD

ADDITIONAL AMENITIES

- [ ] LAUNDRY
- [ ] WI-FI
- [ ] GAME RENTALS
- [ ] FIRE RING
- [ ] CABLE TV
- [ ] HIKING TRAILS
- [ ] SPORT ACTIVITY
- [ ] FITNESS ROOM
- [ ] FISHING
- [ ] POOL
- [ ] CLUBHOUSE
- [ ] BOATING
- [ ] RECEIVES MAIL
- [ ] SHOWERS
- [ ] ON-SITE STORE

NOISE LEVEL
- [ ] ACCEPTABLE
- [ ] UNACCEPTABLE

EXTRA FEES
- [ ] KIDS
- [ ] PETS

CLEANLINESS
- [ ] ACCEPTABLE
- [ ] UNACCEPTABLE

Surprising things we saw

Special events/outings

New acquaintances made

Miscellaneous notes

RV PARK/CAMPGROUND: _____

DATE(S) VISITED: _____

SITE NUMBER: _____

OVERALL RATING ☆☆☆☆☆

BASIC CAMPSITE INFORMATION

- ☐ PULL-THROUGH
- ☐ BACK-IN
- ☐ SECLUDED SITE
- ☐ 50 AMP
- ☐ 30 AMP
- ☐ OPEN SITE
- ☐ WATER
- ☐ SEWER
- ☐ CONCRETE PAD

ADDITIONAL AMENITIES

- ☐ LAUNDRY
- ☐ WI-FI
- ☐ GAME RENTALS
- ☐ FIRE RING
- ☐ CABLE TV
- ☐ HIKING TRAILS
- ☐ SPORT ACTIVITY
- ☐ FITNESS ROOM
- ☐ FISHING
- ☐ POOL
- ☐ CLUBHOUSE
- ☐ BOATING
- ☐ RECEIVES MAIL
- ☐ SHOWERS
- ☐ ON-SITE STORE

NOISE LEVEL
- ☐ ACCEPTABLE
- ☐ UNACCEPTABLE

EXTRA FEES
- ☐ KIDS
- ☐ PETS

CLEANLINESS
- ☐ ACCEPTABLE
- ☐ UNACCEPTABLE

Surprising things we saw

_____
_____
_____
_____
_____
_____
_____
_____
_____
_____

Special events/outings

_____
_____
_____
_____
_____
_____
_____
_____
_____
_____

New acquaintances made

_____
_____
_____
_____
_____
_____
_____
_____
_____
_____

Miscellaneous notes

_____
_____
_____
_____
_____
_____
_____
_____
_____
_____

RV PARK/CAMPGROUND: _____

DATE(S) VISITED: _____

SITE NUMBER: _____

OVERALL RATING ☆ ☆ ☆ ☆ ☆

BASIC CAMPSITE INFORMATION

- [ ] PULL-THROUGH
- [ ] BACK-IN
- [ ] SECLUDED SITE
- [ ] 50 AMP
- [ ] 30 AMP
- [ ] OPEN SITE
- [ ] WATER
- [ ] SEWER
- [ ] CONCRETE PAD

ADDITIONAL AMENITIES

- [ ] LAUNDRY
- [ ] WI-FI
- [ ] GAME RENTALS
- [ ] FIRE RING
- [ ] CABLE TV
- [ ] HIKING TRAILS
- [ ] SPORT ACTIVITY
- [ ] FITNESS ROOM
- [ ] FISHING
- [ ] POOL
- [ ] CLUBHOUSE
- [ ] BOATING
- [ ] RECEIVES MAIL
- [ ] SHOWERS
- [ ] ON-SITE STORE

NOISE LEVEL
- [ ] ACCEPTABLE
- [ ] UNACCEPTABLE

EXTRA FEES
- [ ] KIDS
- [ ] PETS

CLEANLINESS
- [ ] ACCEPTABLE
- [ ] UNACCEPTABLE

Surprising things we saw

_____
_____
_____
_____
_____
_____
_____
_____
_____

Special events/outings

_____
_____
_____
_____
_____
_____
_____
_____
_____

New acquaintances made

_____
_____
_____
_____
_____
_____
_____
_____
_____

Miscellaneous notes

_____
_____
_____
_____
_____
_____
_____
_____
_____

RV PARK/CAMPGROUND: _____
DATE(S) VISITED: _____
SITE NUMBER: _____
OVERALL RATING ☆ ☆ ☆ ☆ ☆

BASIC CAMPSITE INFORMATION

- [ ] PULL-THROUGH
- [ ] BACK-IN
- [ ] SECLUDED SITE
- [ ] 50 AMP
- [ ] 30 AMP
- [ ] OPEN SITE
- [ ] WATER
- [ ] SEWER
- [ ] CONCRETE PAD

ADDITIONAL AMENITIES

- [ ] LAUNDRY
- [ ] WI-FI
- [ ] GAME RENTALS
- [ ] FIRE RING
- [ ] CABLE TV
- [ ] HIKING TRAILS
- [ ] SPORT ACTIVITY
- [ ] FITNESS ROOM
- [ ] FISHING
- [ ] POOL
- [ ] CLUBHOUSE
- [ ] BOATING
- [ ] RECEIVES MAIL
- [ ] SHOWERS
- [ ] ON-SITE STORE

NOISE LEVEL
- [ ] ACCEPTABLE
- [ ] UNACCEPTABLE

EXTRA FEES
- [ ] KIDS
- [ ] PETS

CLEANLINESS
- [ ] ACCEPTABLE
- [ ] UNACCEPTABLE

Surprising things we saw

_____
_____
_____
_____
_____
_____
_____
_____
_____

Special events/outings

_____
_____
_____
_____
_____
_____
_____
_____
_____

New acquaintances made

_____
_____
_____
_____
_____
_____
_____
_____
_____

Miscellaneous notes

_____
_____
_____
_____
_____
_____
_____
_____
_____

RV PARK/CAMPGROUND: _____

DATE(S) VISITED: _____

SITE NUMBER: _____

OVERALL RATING ☆☆☆☆☆

BASIC CAMPSITE INFORMATION

- ☐ PULL-THROUGH
- ☐ BACK-IN
- ☐ SECLUDED SITE
- ☐ 50 AMP
- ☐ 30 AMP
- ☐ OPEN SITE
- ☐ WATER
- ☐ SEWER
- ☐ CONCRETE PAD

ADDITIONAL AMENITIES

- ☐ LAUNDRY
- ☐ WI-FI
- ☐ GAME RENTALS
- ☐ FIRE RING
- ☐ CABLE TV
- ☐ HIKING TRAILS
- ☐ SPORT ACTIVITY
- ☐ FITNESS ROOM
- ☐ FISHING
- ☐ POOL
- ☐ CLUBHOUSE
- ☐ BOATING
- ☐ RECEIVES MAIL
- ☐ SHOWERS
- ☐ ON-SITE STORE

NOISE LEVEL
- ☐ ACCEPTABLE
- ☐ UNACCEPTABLE

EXTRA FEES
- ☐ KIDS
- ☐ PETS

CLEANLINESS
- ☐ ACCEPTABLE
- ☐ UNACCEPTABLE

Surprising things we saw

Special events/outings

New acquaintances made

Miscellaneous notes

RV PARK/CAMPGROUND: _____

DATE(S) VISITED: _____

SITE NUMBER: _____

OVERALL RATING ☆☆☆☆☆

BASIC CAMPSITE INFORMATION

- [ ] PULL-THROUGH
- [ ] BACK-IN
- [ ] SECLUDED SITE
- [ ] 50 AMP
- [ ] 30 AMP
- [ ] OPEN SITE
- [ ] WATER
- [ ] SEWER
- [ ] CONCRETE PAD

ADDITIONAL AMENITIES

- [ ] LAUNDRY
- [ ] WI-FI
- [ ] GAME RENTALS
- [ ] FIRE RING
- [ ] CABLE TV
- [ ] HIKING TRAILS
- [ ] SPORT ACTIVITY
- [ ] FITNESS ROOM
- [ ] FISHING
- [ ] POOL
- [ ] CLUBHOUSE
- [ ] BOATING
- [ ] RECEIVES MAIL
- [ ] SHOWERS
- [ ] ON-SITE STORE

NOISE LEVEL
- [ ] ACCEPTABLE
- [ ] UNACCEPTABLE

EXTRA FEES
- [ ] KIDS
- [ ] PETS

CLEANLINESS
- [ ] ACCEPTABLE
- [ ] UNACCEPTABLE

Surprising things we saw

_____
_____
_____
_____
_____
_____
_____
_____
_____
_____

Special events/outings

_____
_____
_____
_____
_____
_____
_____
_____
_____
_____

New acquaintances made

_____
_____
_____
_____
_____
_____
_____
_____
_____
_____

Miscellaneous notes

_____
_____
_____
_____
_____
_____
_____
_____
_____
_____

RV PARK/CAMPGROUND: _____

DATE(S) VISITED: _____

SITE NUMBER: _____

OVERALL RATING ☆ ☆ ☆ ☆ ☆

BASIC CAMPSITE INFORMATION

- [ ] PULL-THROUGH
- [ ] BACK-IN
- [ ] SECLUDED SITE
- [ ] 50 AMP
- [ ] 30 AMP
- [ ] OPEN SITE
- [ ] WATER
- [ ] SEWER
- [ ] CONCRETE PAD

ADDITIONAL AMENITIES

- [ ] LAUNDRY
- [ ] WI-FI
- [ ] GAME RENTALS
- [ ] FIRE RING
- [ ] CABLE TV
- [ ] HIKING TRAILS
- [ ] SPORT ACTIVITY
- [ ] FITNESS ROOM
- [ ] FISHING
- [ ] POOL
- [ ] CLUBHOUSE
- [ ] BOATING
- [ ] RECEIVES MAIL
- [ ] SHOWERS
- [ ] ON-SITE STORE

NOISE LEVEL
- [ ] ACCEPTABLE
- [ ] UNACCEPTABLE

EXTRA FEES
- [ ] KIDS
- [ ] PETS

CLEANLINESS
- [ ] ACCEPTABLE
- [ ] UNACCEPTABLE

Surprising things we saw

Special events/outings

New acquaintances made

Miscellaneous notes

RV PARK/CAMPGROUND: _____

DATE(S) VISITED: _____

SITE NUMBER: _____

OVERALL RATING ☆ ☆ ☆ ☆ ☆

BASIC CAMPSITE INFORMATION

- [ ] PULL-THROUGH
- [ ] BACK-IN
- [ ] SECLUDED SITE
- [ ] 50 AMP
- [ ] 30 AMP
- [ ] OPEN SITE
- [ ] WATER
- [ ] SEWER
- [ ] CONCRETE PAD

ADDITIONAL AMENITIES

- [ ] LAUNDRY
- [ ] WI-FI
- [ ] GAME RENTALS
- [ ] FIRE RING
- [ ] CABLE TV
- [ ] HIKING TRAILS
- [ ] SPORT ACTIVITY
- [ ] FITNESS ROOM
- [ ] FISHING
- [ ] POOL
- [ ] CLUBHOUSE
- [ ] BOATING
- [ ] RECEIVES MAIL
- [ ] SHOWERS
- [ ] ON-SITE STORE

NOISE LEVEL
- [ ] ACCEPTABLE
- [ ] UNACCEPTABLE

EXTRA FEES
- [ ] KIDS
- [ ] PETS

CLEANLINESS
- [ ] ACCEPTABLE
- [ ] UNACCEPTABLE

Surprising things we saw

Special events/outings

New acquaintances made

Miscellaneous notes

RV PARK/CAMPGROUND: _____

DATE(S) VISITED: _____

SITE NUMBER: _____

OVERALL RATING ☆ ☆ ☆ ☆ ☆

BASIC CAMPSITE INFORMATION

- [ ] PULL-THROUGH
- [ ] BACK-IN
- [ ] SECLUDED SITE
- [ ] 50 AMP
- [ ] 30 AMP
- [ ] OPEN SITE
- [ ] WATER
- [ ] SEWER
- [ ] CONCRETE PAD

ADDITIONAL AMENITIES

- [ ] LAUNDRY
- [ ] WI-FI
- [ ] GAME RENTALS
- [ ] FIRE RING
- [ ] CABLE TV
- [ ] HIKING TRAILS
- [ ] SPORT ACTIVITY
- [ ] FITNESS ROOM
- [ ] FISHING
- [ ] POOL
- [ ] CLUBHOUSE
- [ ] BOATING
- [ ] RECEIVES MAIL
- [ ] SHOWERS
- [ ] ON-SITE STORE

NOISE LEVEL
- [ ] ACCEPTABLE
- [ ] UNACCEPTABLE

EXTRA FEES
- [ ] KIDS
- [ ] PETS

CLEANLINESS
- [ ] ACCEPTABLE
- [ ] UNACCEPTABLE

Surprising things we saw

Special events/outings

New acquaintances made

Miscellaneous notes

RV PARK/CAMPGROUND: _____

DATE(S) VISITED: _____

SITE NUMBER: _____

OVERALL RATING ☆ ☆ ☆ ☆ ☆

BASIC CAMPSITE INFORMATION

- [ ] PULL-THROUGH
- [ ] BACK-IN
- [ ] SECLUDED SITE
- [ ] 50 AMP
- [ ] 30 AMP
- [ ] OPEN SITE
- [ ] WATER
- [ ] SEWER
- [ ] CONCRETE PAD

ADDITIONAL AMENITIES

- [ ] LAUNDRY
- [ ] WI-FI
- [ ] GAME RENTALS
- [ ] FIRE RING
- [ ] CABLE TV
- [ ] HIKING TRAILS
- [ ] SPORT ACTIVITY
- [ ] FITNESS ROOM
- [ ] FISHING
- [ ] POOL
- [ ] CLUBHOUSE
- [ ] BOATING
- [ ] RECEIVES MAIL
- [ ] SHOWERS
- [ ] ON-SITE STORE

NOISE LEVEL
- [ ] ACCEPTABLE
- [ ] UNACCEPTABLE

EXTRA FEES
- [ ] KIDS
- [ ] PETS

CLEANLINESS
- [ ] ACCEPTABLE
- [ ] UNACCEPTABLE

Surprising things we saw

Special events/outings

New acquaintances made

Miscellaneous notes

RV PARK/CAMPGROUND: _____

DATE(S) VISITED: _____

SITE NUMBER: _____

OVERALL RATING ☆☆☆☆☆

BASIC CAMPSITE INFORMATION

- ☐ PULL-THROUGH
- ☐ BACK-IN
- ☐ SECLUDED SITE
- ☐ 50 AMP
- ☐ 30 AMP
- ☐ OPEN SITE
- ☐ WATER
- ☐ SEWER
- ☐ CONCRETE PAD

ADDITIONAL AMENITIES

- ☐ LAUNDRY
- ☐ WI-FI
- ☐ GAME RENTALS
- ☐ FIRE RING
- ☐ CABLE TV
- ☐ HIKING TRAILS
- ☐ SPORT ACTIVITY
- ☐ FITNESS ROOM
- ☐ FISHING
- ☐ POOL
- ☐ CLUBHOUSE
- ☐ BOATING
- ☐ RECEIVES MAIL
- ☐ SHOWERS
- ☐ ON-SITE STORE

NOISE LEVEL
- ☐ ACCEPTABLE
- ☐ UNACCEPTABLE

EXTRA FEES
- ☐ KIDS
- ☐ PETS

CLEANLINESS
- ☐ ACCEPTABLE
- ☐ UNACCEPTABLE

Surprising things we saw

_____
_____
_____
_____
_____
_____
_____
_____

Special events/outings

_____
_____
_____
_____
_____
_____
_____
_____

New acquaintances made

_____
_____
_____
_____
_____
_____
_____
_____

Miscellaneous notes

_____
_____
_____
_____
_____
_____
_____
_____

RV PARK/CAMPGROUND: _____

DATE(S) VISITED: _____

SITE NUMBER: _____

OVERALL RATING ☆ ☆ ☆ ☆ ☆

BASIC CAMPSITE INFORMATION

- [ ] PULL-THROUGH
- [ ] BACK-IN
- [ ] SECLUDED SITE
- [ ] 50 AMP
- [ ] 30 AMP
- [ ] OPEN SITE
- [ ] WATER
- [ ] SEWER
- [ ] CONCRETE PAD

ADDITIONAL AMENITIES

- [ ] LAUNDRY
- [ ] WI-FI
- [ ] GAME RENTALS
- [ ] FIRE RING
- [ ] CABLE TV
- [ ] HIKING TRAILS
- [ ] SPORT ACTIVITY
- [ ] FITNESS ROOM
- [ ] FISHING
- [ ] POOL
- [ ] CLUBHOUSE
- [ ] BOATING
- [ ] RECEIVES MAIL
- [ ] SHOWERS
- [ ] ON-SITE STORE

NOISE LEVEL
- [ ] ACCEPTABLE
- [ ] UNACCEPTABLE

EXTRA FEES
- [ ] KIDS
- [ ] PETS

CLEANLINESS
- [ ] ACCEPTABLE
- [ ] UNACCEPTABLE

Surprising things we saw

_____
_____
_____
_____
_____
_____
_____
_____
_____
_____
_____

Special events/outings

_____
_____
_____
_____
_____
_____
_____
_____
_____
_____
_____

New acquaintances made

_____
_____
_____
_____
_____
_____
_____
_____
_____
_____
_____

Miscellaneous notes

_____
_____
_____
_____
_____
_____
_____
_____
_____
_____
_____

RV PARK/CAMPGROUND: _____
DATE(S) VISITED: _____
SITE NUMBER: _____
OVERALL RATING ☆ ☆ ☆ ☆ ☆

BASIC CAMPSITE INFORMATION

- [ ] PULL-THROUGH
- [ ] BACK-IN
- [ ] SECLUDED SITE
- [ ] 50 AMP
- [ ] 30 AMP
- [ ] OPEN SITE
- [ ] WATER
- [ ] SEWER
- [ ] CONCRETE PAD

ADDITIONAL AMENITIES

- [ ] LAUNDRY
- [ ] WI-FI
- [ ] GAME RENTALS
- [ ] FIRE RING
- [ ] CABLE TV
- [ ] HIKING TRAILS
- [ ] SPORT ACTIVITY
- [ ] FITNESS ROOM
- [ ] FISHING
- [ ] POOL
- [ ] CLUBHOUSE
- [ ] BOATING
- [ ] RECEIVES MAIL
- [ ] SHOWERS
- [ ] ON-SITE STORE

NOISE LEVEL
- [ ] ACCEPTABLE
- [ ] UNACCEPTABLE

EXTRA FEES
- [ ] KIDS
- [ ] PETS

CLEANLINESS
- [ ] ACCEPTABLE
- [ ] UNACCEPTABLE

Surprising things we saw

_____
_____
_____
_____
_____
_____
_____
_____
_____

Special events/outings

_____
_____
_____
_____
_____
_____
_____
_____
_____

New acquaintances made

_____
_____
_____
_____
_____
_____
_____
_____
_____

Miscellaneous notes

_____
_____
_____
_____
_____
_____
_____
_____
_____

RV PARK/CAMPGROUND: _____

DATE(S) VISITED: _____

SITE NUMBER: _____

OVERALL RATING ☆ ☆ ☆ ☆ ☆

BASIC CAMPSITE INFORMATION

- [ ] PULL-THROUGH
- [ ] BACK-IN
- [ ] SECLUDED SITE
- [ ] 50 AMP
- [ ] 30 AMP
- [ ] OPEN SITE
- [ ] WATER
- [ ] SEWER
- [ ] CONCRETE PAD

ADDITIONAL AMENITIES

- [ ] LAUNDRY
- [ ] WI-FI
- [ ] GAME RENTALS
- [ ] FIRE RING
- [ ] CABLE TV
- [ ] HIKING TRAILS
- [ ] SPORT ACTIVITY
- [ ] FITNESS ROOM
- [ ] FISHING
- [ ] POOL
- [ ] CLUBHOUSE
- [ ] BOATING
- [ ] RECEIVES MAIL
- [ ] SHOWERS
- [ ] ON-SITE STORE

NOISE LEVEL
- [ ] ACCEPTABLE
- [ ] UNACCEPTABLE

EXTRA FEES
- [ ] KIDS
- [ ] PETS

CLEANLINESS
- [ ] ACCEPTABLE
- [ ] UNACCEPTABLE

Surprising things we saw

_____
_____
_____
_____
_____
_____
_____
_____
_____

Special events/outings

_____
_____
_____
_____
_____
_____
_____
_____
_____

New acquaintances made

_____
_____
_____
_____
_____
_____
_____
_____
_____

Miscellaneous notes

_____
_____
_____
_____
_____
_____
_____
_____
_____

RV PARK/CAMPGROUND: _____

DATE(S) VISITED: _____

SITE NUMBER: _____

OVERALL RATING ☆ ☆ ☆ ☆ ☆

BASIC CAMPSITE INFORMATION

- ☐ PULL-THROUGH
- ☐ BACK-IN
- ☐ SECLUDED SITE
- ☐ 50 AMP
- ☐ 30 AMP
- ☐ OPEN SITE
- ☐ WATER
- ☐ SEWER
- ☐ CONCRETE PAD

ADDITIONAL AMENITIES

- ☐ LAUNDRY
- ☐ WI-FI
- ☐ GAME RENTALS
- ☐ FIRE RING
- ☐ CABLE TV
- ☐ HIKING TRAILS
- ☐ SPORT ACTIVITY
- ☐ FITNESS ROOM
- ☐ FISHING
- ☐ POOL
- ☐ CLUBHOUSE
- ☐ BOATING
- ☐ RECEIVES MAIL
- ☐ SHOWERS
- ☐ ON-SITE STORE

NOISE LEVEL
- ☐ ACCEPTABLE
- ☐ UNACCEPTABLE

EXTRA FEES
- ☐ KIDS
- ☐ PETS

CLEANLINESS
- ☐ ACCEPTABLE
- ☐ UNACCEPTABLE

Surprising things we saw

Special events/outings

New acquaintances made

Miscellaneous notes

RV PARK/CAMPGROUND: _____
DATE(S) VISITED: _____
SITE NUMBER: _____
OVERALL RATING ☆ ☆ ☆ ☆ ☆

BASIC CAMPSITE INFORMATION

- [ ] PULL-THROUGH
- [ ] BACK-IN
- [ ] SECLUDED SITE
- [ ] 50 AMP
- [ ] 30 AMP
- [ ] OPEN SITE
- [ ] WATER
- [ ] SEWER
- [ ] CONCRETE PAD

ADDITIONAL AMENITIES

- [ ] LAUNDRY
- [ ] WI-FI
- [ ] GAME RENTALS
- [ ] FIRE RING
- [ ] CABLE TV
- [ ] HIKING TRAILS
- [ ] SPORT ACTIVITY
- [ ] FITNESS ROOM
- [ ] FISHING
- [ ] POOL
- [ ] CLUBHOUSE
- [ ] BOATING
- [ ] RECEIVES MAIL
- [ ] SHOWERS
- [ ] ON-SITE STORE

NOISE LEVEL
- [ ] ACCEPTABLE
- [ ] UNACCEPTABLE

EXTRA FEES
- [ ] KIDS
- [ ] PETS

CLEANLINESS
- [ ] ACCEPTABLE
- [ ] UNACCEPTABLE

Surprising things we saw

_____
_____
_____
_____
_____
_____
_____
_____
_____
_____

Special events/outings

_____
_____
_____
_____
_____
_____
_____
_____
_____
_____

New acquaintances made

_____
_____
_____
_____
_____
_____
_____
_____
_____
_____

Miscellaneous notes

_____
_____
_____
_____
_____
_____
_____
_____
_____
_____

RV PARK/CAMPGROUND: _____
DATE(S) VISITED: _____
SITE NUMBER: _____
OVERALL RATING ☆☆☆☆☆

BASIC CAMPSITE INFORMATION

- [ ] PULL-THROUGH
- [ ] BACK-IN
- [ ] SECLUDED SITE
- [ ] 50 AMP
- [ ] 30 AMP
- [ ] OPEN SITE
- [ ] WATER
- [ ] SEWER
- [ ] CONCRETE PAD

ADDITIONAL AMENITIES

- [ ] LAUNDRY
- [ ] WI-FI
- [ ] GAME RENTALS
- [ ] FIRE RING
- [ ] CABLE TV
- [ ] HIKING TRAILS
- [ ] SPORT ACTIVITY
- [ ] FITNESS ROOM
- [ ] FISHING
- [ ] POOL
- [ ] CLUBHOUSE
- [ ] BOATING
- [ ] RECEIVES MAIL
- [ ] SHOWERS
- [ ] ON-SITE STORE

NOISE LEVEL
- [ ] ACCEPTABLE
- [ ] UNACCEPTABLE

EXTRA FEES
- [ ] KIDS
- [ ] PETS

CLEANLINESS
- [ ] ACCEPTABLE
- [ ] UNACCEPTABLE

Surprising things we saw

_____
_____
_____
_____
_____
_____
_____
_____
_____
_____

Special events/outings

_____
_____
_____
_____
_____
_____
_____
_____
_____
_____

New acquaintances made

_____
_____
_____
_____
_____
_____
_____
_____
_____
_____

Miscellaneous notes

_____
_____
_____
_____
_____
_____
_____
_____
_____
_____

RV PARK/CAMPGROUND: _____

DATE(S) VISITED: _____

SITE NUMBER: _____

OVERALL RATING ☆ ☆ ☆ ☆ ☆

BASIC CAMPSITE INFORMATION

- [ ] PULL-THROUGH
- [ ] BACK-IN
- [ ] SECLUDED SITE
- [ ] 50 AMP
- [ ] 30 AMP
- [ ] OPEN SITE
- [ ] WATER
- [ ] SEWER
- [ ] CONCRETE PAD

ADDITIONAL AMENITIES

- [ ] LAUNDRY
- [ ] WI-FI
- [ ] GAME RENTALS
- [ ] FIRE RING
- [ ] CABLE TV
- [ ] HIKING TRAILS
- [ ] SPORT ACTIVITY
- [ ] FITNESS ROOM
- [ ] FISHING
- [ ] POOL
- [ ] CLUBHOUSE
- [ ] BOATING
- [ ] RECEIVES MAIL
- [ ] SHOWERS
- [ ] ON-SITE STORE

NOISE LEVEL
- [ ] ACCEPTABLE
- [ ] UNACCEPTABLE

EXTRA FEES
- [ ] KIDS
- [ ] PETS

CLEANLINESS
- [ ] ACCEPTABLE
- [ ] UNACCEPTABLE

Surprising things we saw

_____
_____
_____
_____
_____
_____
_____
_____
_____
_____

Special events/outings

_____
_____
_____
_____
_____
_____
_____
_____
_____
_____

New acquaintances made

_____
_____
_____
_____
_____
_____
_____
_____
_____
_____

Miscellaneous notes

_____
_____
_____
_____
_____
_____
_____
_____
_____
_____

RV PARK/CAMPGROUND: _____

DATE(S) VISITED: _____

SITE NUMBER: _____

OVERALL RATING ☆☆☆☆☆

BASIC CAMPSITE INFORMATION

- [ ] PULL-THROUGH
- [ ] BACK-IN
- [ ] SECLUDED SITE
- [ ] 50 AMP
- [ ] 30 AMP
- [ ] OPEN SITE
- [ ] WATER
- [ ] SEWER
- [ ] CONCRETE PAD

ADDITIONAL AMENITIES

- [ ] LAUNDRY
- [ ] WI-FI
- [ ] GAME RENTALS
- [ ] FIRE RING
- [ ] CABLE TV
- [ ] HIKING TRAILS
- [ ] SPORT ACTIVITY
- [ ] FITNESS ROOM
- [ ] FISHING
- [ ] POOL
- [ ] CLUBHOUSE
- [ ] BOATING
- [ ] RECEIVES MAIL
- [ ] SHOWERS
- [ ] ON-SITE STORE

NOISE LEVEL
- [ ] ACCEPTABLE
- [ ] UNACCEPTABLE

EXTRA FEES
- [ ] KIDS
- [ ] PETS

CLEANLINESS
- [ ] ACCEPTABLE
- [ ] UNACCEPTABLE

Surprising things we saw

_____
_____
_____
_____
_____
_____
_____
_____
_____

Special events/outings

_____
_____
_____
_____
_____
_____
_____
_____
_____

New acquaintances made

_____
_____
_____
_____
_____
_____
_____
_____
_____

Miscellaneous notes

_____
_____
_____
_____
_____
_____
_____
_____
_____

RV PARK/CAMPGROUND: _____

DATE(S) VISITED: _____

SITE NUMBER: _____

OVERALL RATING ☆ ☆ ☆ ☆ ☆

BASIC CAMPSITE INFORMATION

- [ ] PULL-THROUGH
- [ ] BACK-IN
- [ ] SECLUDED SITE
- [ ] 50 AMP
- [ ] 30 AMP
- [ ] OPEN SITE
- [ ] WATER
- [ ] SEWER
- [ ] CONCRETE PAD

ADDITIONAL AMENITIES

- [ ] LAUNDRY
- [ ] WI-FI
- [ ] GAME RENTALS
- [ ] FIRE RING
- [ ] CABLE TV
- [ ] HIKING TRAILS
- [ ] SPORT ACTIVITY
- [ ] FITNESS ROOM
- [ ] FISHING
- [ ] POOL
- [ ] CLUBHOUSE
- [ ] BOATING
- [ ] RECEIVES MAIL
- [ ] SHOWERS
- [ ] ON-SITE STORE

NOISE LEVEL
- [ ] ACCEPTABLE
- [ ] UNACCEPTABLE

EXTRA FEES
- [ ] KIDS
- [ ] PETS

CLEANLINESS
- [ ] ACCEPTABLE
- [ ] UNACCEPTABLE

Surprising things we saw

Special events/outings

New acquaintances made

Miscellaneous notes

RV PARK/CAMPGROUND: _____

DATE(S) VISITED: _____

SITE NUMBER: _____

OVERALL RATING ☆ ☆ ☆ ☆ ☆

BASIC CAMPSITE INFORMATION

- [ ] PULL-THROUGH
- [ ] BACK-IN
- [ ] SECLUDED SITE
- [ ] 50 AMP
- [ ] 30 AMP
- [ ] OPEN SITE
- [ ] WATER
- [ ] SEWER
- [ ] CONCRETE PAD

ADDITIONAL AMENITIES

- [ ] LAUNDRY
- [ ] WI-FI
- [ ] GAME RENTALS
- [ ] FIRE RING
- [ ] CABLE TV
- [ ] HIKING TRAILS
- [ ] SPORT ACTIVITY
- [ ] FITNESS ROOM
- [ ] FISHING
- [ ] POOL
- [ ] CLUBHOUSE
- [ ] BOATING
- [ ] RECEIVES MAIL
- [ ] SHOWERS
- [ ] ON-SITE STORE

NOISE LEVEL
- [ ] ACCEPTABLE
- [ ] UNACCEPTABLE

EXTRA FEES
- [ ] KIDS
- [ ] PETS

CLEANLINESS
- [ ] ACCEPTABLE
- [ ] UNACCEPTABLE

Surprising things we saw

Special events/outings

New acquaintances made

Miscellaneous notes

RV PARK/CAMPGROUND: _____
DATE(S) VISITED: _____
SITE NUMBER: _____
OVERALL RATING ☆☆☆☆☆

BASIC CAMPSITE INFORMATION

- [ ] PULL-THROUGH
- [ ] BACK-IN
- [ ] SECLUDED SITE
- [ ] 50 AMP
- [ ] 30 AMP
- [ ] OPEN SITE
- [ ] WATER
- [ ] SEWER
- [ ] CONCRETE PAD

ADDITIONAL AMENITIES

- [ ] LAUNDRY
- [ ] WI-FI
- [ ] GAME RENTALS
- [ ] FIRE RING
- [ ] CABLE TV
- [ ] HIKING TRAILS
- [ ] SPORT ACTIVITY
- [ ] FITNESS ROOM
- [ ] FISHING
- [ ] POOL
- [ ] CLUBHOUSE
- [ ] BOATING
- [ ] RECEIVES MAIL
- [ ] SHOWERS
- [ ] ON-SITE STORE

NOISE LEVEL
- [ ] ACCEPTABLE
- [ ] UNACCEPTABLE

EXTRA FEES
- [ ] KIDS
- [ ] PETS

CLEANLINESS
- [ ] ACCEPTABLE
- [ ] UNACCEPTABLE

Surprising things we saw

_____
_____
_____
_____
_____
_____
_____
_____
_____
_____

Special events/outings

_____
_____
_____
_____
_____
_____
_____
_____
_____
_____

New acquaintances made

_____
_____
_____
_____
_____
_____
_____
_____
_____
_____

Miscellaneous notes

_____
_____
_____
_____
_____
_____
_____
_____
_____
_____

RV PARK/CAMPGROUND: _____
DATE(S) VISITED: _____
SITE NUMBER: _____
OVERALL RATING ☆ ☆ ☆ ☆ ☆

BASIC CAMPSITE INFORMATION

- [ ] PULL-THROUGH
- [ ] BACK-IN
- [ ] SECLUDED SITE
- [ ] 50 AMP
- [ ] 30 AMP
- [ ] OPEN SITE
- [ ] WATER
- [ ] SEWER
- [ ] CONCRETE PAD

ADDITIONAL AMENITIES

- [ ] LAUNDRY
- [ ] WI-FI
- [ ] GAME RENTALS
- [ ] FIRE RING
- [ ] CABLE TV
- [ ] HIKING TRAILS
- [ ] SPORT ACTIVITY
- [ ] FITNESS ROOM
- [ ] FISHING
- [ ] POOL
- [ ] CLUBHOUSE
- [ ] BOATING
- [ ] RECEIVES MAIL
- [ ] SHOWERS
- [ ] ON-SITE STORE

NOISE LEVEL
- [ ] ACCEPTABLE
- [ ] UNACCEPTABLE

EXTRA FEES
- [ ] KIDS
- [ ] PETS

CLEANLINESS
- [ ] ACCEPTABLE
- [ ] UNACCEPTABLE

Surprising things we saw

_____
_____
_____
_____
_____
_____
_____
_____
_____
_____

Special events/outings

_____
_____
_____
_____
_____
_____
_____
_____
_____
_____

New acquaintances made

_____
_____
_____
_____
_____
_____
_____
_____
_____
_____

Miscellaneous notes

_____
_____
_____
_____
_____
_____
_____
_____
_____
_____

RV PARK/CAMPGROUND: _____
DATE(S) VISITED: _____
SITE NUMBER: _____
OVERALL RATING ☆ ☆ ☆ ☆ ☆

BASIC CAMPSITE INFORMATION

- [ ] PULL-THROUGH
- [ ] BACK-IN
- [ ] SECLUDED SITE
- [ ] 50 AMP
- [ ] 30 AMP
- [ ] OPEN SITE
- [ ] WATER
- [ ] SEWER
- [ ] CONCRETE PAD

ADDITIONAL AMENITIES

- [ ] LAUNDRY
- [ ] WI-FI
- [ ] GAME RENTALS
- [ ] FIRE RING
- [ ] CABLE TV
- [ ] HIKING TRAILS
- [ ] SPORT ACTIVITY
- [ ] FITNESS ROOM
- [ ] FISHING
- [ ] POOL
- [ ] CLUBHOUSE
- [ ] BOATING
- [ ] RECEIVES MAIL
- [ ] SHOWERS
- [ ] ON-SITE STORE

NOISE LEVEL
- [ ] ACCEPTABLE
- [ ] UNACCEPTABLE

EXTRA FEES
- [ ] KIDS
- [ ] PETS

CLEANLINESS
- [ ] ACCEPTABLE
- [ ] UNACCEPTABLE

Surprising things we saw

_____
_____
_____
_____
_____
_____
_____
_____
_____
_____
_____

Special events/outings

_____
_____
_____
_____
_____
_____
_____
_____
_____
_____
_____

New acquaintances made

_____
_____
_____
_____
_____
_____
_____
_____
_____
_____
_____

Miscellaneous notes

_____
_____
_____
_____
_____
_____
_____
_____
_____
_____
_____

RV PARK/CAMPGROUND: _____
DATE(S) VISITED: _____
SITE NUMBER: _____
OVERALL RATING ☆ ☆ ☆ ☆ ☆

BASIC CAMPSITE INFORMATION

- [ ] PULL-THROUGH
- [ ] BACK-IN
- [ ] SECLUDED SITE
- [ ] 50 AMP
- [ ] 30 AMP
- [ ] OPEN SITE
- [ ] WATER
- [ ] SEWER
- [ ] CONCRETE PAD

ADDITIONAL AMENITIES

- [ ] LAUNDRY
- [ ] WI-FI
- [ ] GAME RENTALS
- [ ] FIRE RING
- [ ] CABLE TV
- [ ] HIKING TRAILS
- [ ] SPORT ACTIVITY
- [ ] FITNESS ROOM
- [ ] FISHING
- [ ] POOL
- [ ] CLUBHOUSE
- [ ] BOATING
- [ ] RECEIVES MAIL
- [ ] SHOWERS
- [ ] ON-SITE STORE

NOISE LEVEL
- [ ] ACCEPTABLE
- [ ] UNACCEPTABLE

EXTRA FEES
- [ ] KIDS
- [ ] PETS

CLEANLINESS
- [ ] ACCEPTABLE
- [ ] UNACCEPTABLE

Surprising things we saw

Special events/outings

New acquaintances made

Miscellaneous notes

RV PARK/CAMPGROUND: _____
DATE(S) VISITED: _____
SITE NUMBER: _____
OVERALL RATING ☆☆☆☆☆

BASIC CAMPSITE INFORMATION

- [ ] PULL-THROUGH
- [ ] BACK-IN
- [ ] SECLUDED SITE
- [ ] 50 AMP
- [ ] 30 AMP
- [ ] OPEN SITE
- [ ] WATER
- [ ] SEWER
- [ ] CONCRETE PAD

ADDITIONAL AMENITIES

- [ ] LAUNDRY
- [ ] WI-FI
- [ ] GAME RENTALS
- [ ] FIRE RING
- [ ] CABLE TV
- [ ] HIKING TRAILS
- [ ] SPORT ACTIVITY
- [ ] FITNESS ROOM
- [ ] FISHING
- [ ] POOL
- [ ] CLUBHOUSE
- [ ] BOATING
- [ ] RECEIVES MAIL
- [ ] SHOWERS
- [ ] ON-SITE STORE

NOISE LEVEL
- [ ] ACCEPTABLE
- [ ] UNACCEPTABLE

EXTRA FEES
- [ ] KIDS
- [ ] PETS

CLEANLINESS
- [ ] ACCEPTABLE
- [ ] UNACCEPTABLE

Surprising things we saw

Special events/outings

New acquaintances made

Miscellaneous notes

RV PARK/CAMPGROUND: _____

DATE(S) VISITED: _____

SITE NUMBER: _____

OVERALL RATING ☆ ☆ ☆ ☆ ☆

BASIC CAMPSITE INFORMATION

- [ ] PULL-THROUGH
- [ ] BACK-IN
- [ ] SECLUDED SITE
- [ ] 50 AMP
- [ ] 30 AMP
- [ ] OPEN SITE
- [ ] WATER
- [ ] SEWER
- [ ] CONCRETE PAD

ADDITIONAL AMENITIES

- [ ] LAUNDRY
- [ ] WI-FI
- [ ] GAME RENTALS
- [ ] FIRE RING
- [ ] CABLE TV
- [ ] HIKING TRAILS
- [ ] SPORT ACTIVITY
- [ ] FITNESS ROOM
- [ ] FISHING
- [ ] POOL
- [ ] CLUBHOUSE
- [ ] BOATING
- [ ] RECEIVES MAIL
- [ ] SHOWERS
- [ ] ON-SITE STORE

NOISE LEVEL
- [ ] ACCEPTABLE
- [ ] UNACCEPTABLE

EXTRA FEES
- [ ] KIDS
- [ ] PETS

CLEANLINESS
- [ ] ACCEPTABLE
- [ ] UNACCEPTABLE

Surprising things we saw

Special events/outings

New acquaintances made

Miscellaneous notes

RV PARK/CAMPGROUND: _____

DATE(S) VISITED: _____

SITE NUMBER: _____

OVERALL RATING ☆ ☆ ☆ ☆ ☆

BASIC CAMPSITE INFORMATION

- [ ] PULL-THROUGH
- [ ] BACK-IN
- [ ] SECLUDED SITE
- [ ] 50 AMP
- [ ] 30 AMP
- [ ] OPEN SITE
- [ ] WATER
- [ ] SEWER
- [ ] CONCRETE PAD

ADDITIONAL AMENITIES

- [ ] LAUNDRY
- [ ] WI-FI
- [ ] GAME RENTALS
- [ ] FIRE RING
- [ ] CABLE TV
- [ ] HIKING TRAILS
- [ ] SPORT ACTIVITY
- [ ] FITNESS ROOM
- [ ] FISHING
- [ ] POOL
- [ ] CLUBHOUSE
- [ ] BOATING
- [ ] RECEIVES MAIL
- [ ] SHOWERS
- [ ] ON-SITE STORE

NOISE LEVEL
- [ ] ACCEPTABLE
- [ ] UNACCEPTABLE

EXTRA FEES
- [ ] KIDS
- [ ] PETS

CLEANLINESS
- [ ] ACCEPTABLE
- [ ] UNACCEPTABLE

Surprising things we saw

Special events/outings

New acquaintances made

Miscellaneous notes

RV PARK/CAMPGROUND: _____

DATE(S) VISITED: _____

SITE NUMBER: _____

OVERALL RATING ☆ ☆ ☆ ☆ ☆

BASIC CAMPSITE INFORMATION

- [ ] PULL-THROUGH
- [ ] BACK-IN
- [ ] SECLUDED SITE
- [ ] 50 AMP
- [ ] 30 AMP
- [ ] OPEN SITE
- [ ] WATER
- [ ] SEWER
- [ ] CONCRETE PAD

ADDITIONAL AMENITIES

- [ ] LAUNDRY
- [ ] WI-FI
- [ ] GAME RENTALS
- [ ] FIRE RING
- [ ] CABLE TV
- [ ] HIKING TRAILS
- [ ] SPORT ACTIVITY
- [ ] FITNESS ROOM
- [ ] FISHING
- [ ] POOL
- [ ] CLUBHOUSE
- [ ] BOATING
- [ ] RECEIVES MAIL
- [ ] SHOWERS
- [ ] ON-SITE STORE

NOISE LEVEL
- [ ] ACCEPTABLE
- [ ] UNACCEPTABLE

EXTRA FEES
- [ ] KIDS
- [ ] PETS

CLEANLINESS
- [ ] ACCEPTABLE
- [ ] UNACCEPTABLE

Surprising things we saw

Special events/outings

New acquaintances made

Miscellaneous notes

RV PARK/CAMPGROUND: _____

DATE(S) VISITED: _____

SITE NUMBER: _____

OVERALL RATING ☆ ☆ ☆ ☆ ☆

BASIC CAMPSITE INFORMATION

- [ ] PULL-THROUGH
- [ ] BACK-IN
- [ ] SECLUDED SITE
- [ ] 50 AMP
- [ ] 30 AMP
- [ ] OPEN SITE
- [ ] WATER
- [ ] SEWER
- [ ] CONCRETE PAD

ADDITIONAL AMENITIES

- [ ] LAUNDRY
- [ ] WI-FI
- [ ] GAME RENTALS
- [ ] FIRE RING
- [ ] CABLE TV
- [ ] HIKING TRAILS
- [ ] SPORT ACTIVITY
- [ ] FITNESS ROOM
- [ ] FISHING
- [ ] POOL
- [ ] CLUBHOUSE
- [ ] BOATING
- [ ] RECEIVES MAIL
- [ ] SHOWERS
- [ ] ON-SITE STORE

NOISE LEVEL
- [ ] ACCEPTABLE
- [ ] UNACCEPTABLE

EXTRA FEES
- [ ] KIDS
- [ ] PETS

CLEANLINESS
- [ ] ACCEPTABLE
- [ ] UNACCEPTABLE

Surprising things we saw

Special events/outings

New acquaintances made

Miscellaneous notes

RV PARK/CAMPGROUND: _____
DATE(S) VISITED: _____
SITE NUMBER: _____
OVERALL RATING ☆ ☆ ☆ ☆ ☆

BASIC CAMPSITE INFORMATION

- [ ] PULL-THROUGH
- [ ] BACK-IN
- [ ] SECLUDED SITE
- [ ] 50 AMP
- [ ] 30 AMP
- [ ] OPEN SITE
- [ ] WATER
- [ ] SEWER
- [ ] CONCRETE PAD

ADDITIONAL AMENITIES

- [ ] LAUNDRY
- [ ] WI-FI
- [ ] GAME RENTALS
- [ ] FIRE RING
- [ ] CABLE TV
- [ ] HIKING TRAILS
- [ ] SPORT ACTIVITY
- [ ] FITNESS ROOM
- [ ] FISHING
- [ ] POOL
- [ ] CLUBHOUSE
- [ ] BOATING
- [ ] RECEIVES MAIL
- [ ] SHOWERS
- [ ] ON-SITE STORE

NOISE LEVEL
- [ ] ACCEPTABLE
- [ ] UNACCEPTABLE

EXTRA FEES
- [ ] KIDS
- [ ] PETS

CLEANLINESS
- [ ] ACCEPTABLE
- [ ] UNACCEPTABLE

Surprising things we saw

_____
_____
_____
_____
_____
_____
_____
_____
_____
_____

Special events/outings

_____
_____
_____
_____
_____
_____
_____
_____
_____
_____

New acquaintances made

_____
_____
_____
_____
_____
_____
_____
_____
_____
_____

Miscellaneous notes

_____
_____
_____
_____
_____
_____
_____
_____
_____
_____

RV PARK/CAMPGROUND: _____
DATE(S) VISITED: _____
SITE NUMBER: _____
OVERALL RATING ☆ ☆ ☆ ☆ ☆

BASIC CAMPSITE INFORMATION

- [ ] PULL-THROUGH
- [ ] BACK-IN
- [ ] SECLUDED SITE
- [ ] 50 AMP
- [ ] 30 AMP
- [ ] OPEN SITE
- [ ] WATER
- [ ] SEWER
- [ ] CONCRETE PAD

ADDITIONAL AMENITIES

- [ ] LAUNDRY
- [ ] WI-FI
- [ ] GAME RENTALS
- [ ] FIRE RING
- [ ] CABLE TV
- [ ] HIKING TRAILS
- [ ] SPORT ACTIVITY
- [ ] FITNESS ROOM
- [ ] FISHING
- [ ] POOL
- [ ] CLUBHOUSE
- [ ] BOATING
- [ ] RECEIVES MAIL
- [ ] SHOWERS
- [ ] ON-SITE STORE

NOISE LEVEL
- [ ] ACCEPTABLE
- [ ] UNACCEPTABLE

EXTRA FEES
- [ ] KIDS
- [ ] PETS

CLEANLINESS
- [ ] ACCEPTABLE
- [ ] UNACCEPTABLE

Surprising things we saw

Special events/outings

New acquaintances made

Miscellaneous notes

RV PARK/CAMPGROUND: _____
DATE(S) VISITED: _____
SITE NUMBER: _____
OVERALL RATING ☆☆☆☆☆

BASIC CAMPSITE INFORMATION

- [ ] PULL-THROUGH
- [ ] BACK-IN
- [ ] SECLUDED SITE
- [ ] 50 AMP
- [ ] 30 AMP
- [ ] OPEN SITE
- [ ] WATER
- [ ] SEWER
- [ ] CONCRETE PAD

ADDITIONAL AMENITIES

- [ ] LAUNDRY
- [ ] WI-FI
- [ ] GAME RENTALS
- [ ] FIRE RING
- [ ] CABLE TV
- [ ] HIKING TRAILS
- [ ] SPORT ACTIVITY
- [ ] FITNESS ROOM
- [ ] FISHING
- [ ] POOL
- [ ] CLUBHOUSE
- [ ] BOATING
- [ ] RECEIVES MAIL
- [ ] SHOWERS
- [ ] ON-SITE STORE

NOISE LEVEL
- [ ] ACCEPTABLE
- [ ] UNACCEPTABLE

EXTRA FEES
- [ ] KIDS
- [ ] PETS

CLEANLINESS
- [ ] ACCEPTABLE
- [ ] UNACCEPTABLE

Surprising things we saw

_____
_____
_____
_____
_____
_____
_____
_____

Special events/outings

_____
_____
_____
_____
_____
_____
_____
_____

New acquaintances made

_____
_____
_____
_____
_____
_____
_____
_____

Miscellaneous notes

_____
_____
_____
_____
_____
_____
_____
_____

RV PARK/CAMPGROUND: _____
DATE(S) VISITED: _____
SITE NUMBER: _____
OVERALL RATING ☆ ☆ ☆ ☆ ☆

BASIC CAMPSITE INFORMATION

- [ ] PULL-THROUGH
- [ ] BACK-IN
- [ ] SECLUDED SITE
- [ ] 50 AMP
- [ ] 30 AMP
- [ ] OPEN SITE
- [ ] WATER
- [ ] SEWER
- [ ] CONCRETE PAD

ADDITIONAL AMENITIES

- [ ] LAUNDRY
- [ ] WI-FI
- [ ] GAME RENTALS
- [ ] FIRE RING
- [ ] CABLE TV
- [ ] HIKING TRAILS
- [ ] SPORT ACTIVITY
- [ ] FITNESS ROOM
- [ ] FISHING
- [ ] POOL
- [ ] CLUBHOUSE
- [ ] BOATING
- [ ] RECEIVES MAIL
- [ ] SHOWERS
- [ ] ON-SITE STORE

NOISE LEVEL
- [ ] ACCEPTABLE
- [ ] UNACCEPTABLE

EXTRA FEES
- [ ] KIDS
- [ ] PETS

CLEANLINESS
- [ ] ACCEPTABLE
- [ ] UNACCEPTABLE

Surprising things we saw

Special events/outings

New acquaintances made

Miscellaneous notes

RV PARK/CAMPGROUND: _____

DATE(S) VISITED: _____

SITE NUMBER: _____

OVERALL RATING ☆ ☆ ☆ ☆ ☆

BASIC CAMPSITE INFORMATION

- [ ] PULL-THROUGH
- [ ] BACK-IN
- [ ] SECLUDED SITE
- [ ] 50 AMP
- [ ] 30 AMP
- [ ] OPEN SITE
- [ ] WATER
- [ ] SEWER
- [ ] CONCRETE PAD

ADDITIONAL AMENITIES

- [ ] LAUNDRY
- [ ] WI-FI
- [ ] GAME RENTALS
- [ ] FIRE RING
- [ ] CABLE TV
- [ ] HIKING TRAILS
- [ ] SPORT ACTIVITY
- [ ] FITNESS ROOM
- [ ] FISHING
- [ ] POOL
- [ ] CLUBHOUSE
- [ ] BOATING
- [ ] RECEIVES MAIL
- [ ] SHOWERS
- [ ] ON-SITE STORE

NOISE LEVEL
- [ ] ACCEPTABLE
- [ ] UNACCEPTABLE

EXTRA FEES
- [ ] KIDS
- [ ] PETS

CLEANLINESS
- [ ] ACCEPTABLE
- [ ] UNACCEPTABLE

Surprising things we saw

Special events/outings

New acquaintances made

Miscellaneous notes

RV PARK/CAMPGROUND: _____

DATE(S) VISITED: _____

SITE NUMBER: _____

OVERALL RATING ☆ ☆ ☆ ☆ ☆

BASIC CAMPSITE INFORMATION

- [ ] PULL-THROUGH
- [ ] BACK-IN
- [ ] SECLUDED SITE
- [ ] 50 AMP
- [ ] 30 AMP
- [ ] OPEN SITE
- [ ] WATER
- [ ] SEWER
- [ ] CONCRETE PAD

ADDITIONAL AMENITIES

- [ ] LAUNDRY
- [ ] WI-FI
- [ ] GAME RENTALS
- [ ] FIRE RING
- [ ] CABLE TV
- [ ] HIKING TRAILS
- [ ] SPORT ACTIVITY
- [ ] FITNESS ROOM
- [ ] FISHING
- [ ] POOL
- [ ] CLUBHOUSE
- [ ] BOATING
- [ ] RECEIVES MAIL
- [ ] SHOWERS
- [ ] ON-SITE STORE

NOISE LEVEL
- [ ] ACCEPTABLE
- [ ] UNACCEPTABLE

EXTRA FEES
- [ ] KIDS
- [ ] PETS

CLEANLINESS
- [ ] ACCEPTABLE
- [ ] UNACCEPTABLE

Surprising things we saw

_____
_____
_____
_____
_____
_____
_____
_____
_____
_____

Special events/outings

_____
_____
_____
_____
_____
_____
_____
_____
_____
_____

New acquaintances made

_____
_____
_____
_____
_____
_____
_____
_____
_____
_____

Miscellaneous notes

_____
_____
_____
_____
_____
_____
_____
_____
_____
_____

RV PARK/CAMPGROUND: _____

DATE(S) VISITED: _____

SITE NUMBER: _____

OVERALL RATING ☆ ☆ ☆ ☆ ☆

BASIC CAMPSITE INFORMATION

- [ ] PULL-THROUGH
- [ ] BACK-IN
- [ ] SECLUDED SITE
- [ ] 50 AMP
- [ ] 30 AMP
- [ ] OPEN SITE
- [ ] WATER
- [ ] SEWER
- [ ] CONCRETE PAD

ADDITIONAL AMENITIES

- [ ] LAUNDRY
- [ ] WI-FI
- [ ] GAME RENTALS
- [ ] FIRE RING
- [ ] CABLE TV
- [ ] HIKING TRAILS
- [ ] SPORT ACTIVITY
- [ ] FITNESS ROOM
- [ ] FISHING
- [ ] POOL
- [ ] CLUBHOUSE
- [ ] BOATING
- [ ] RECEIVES MAIL
- [ ] SHOWERS
- [ ] ON-SITE STORE

NOISE LEVEL
- [ ] ACCEPTABLE
- [ ] UNACCEPTABLE

EXTRA FEES
- [ ] KIDS
- [ ] PETS

CLEANLINESS
- [ ] ACCEPTABLE
- [ ] UNACCEPTABLE

Surprising things we saw

_____
_____
_____
_____
_____
_____
_____
_____
_____
_____

Special events/outings

_____
_____
_____
_____
_____
_____
_____
_____
_____
_____

New acquaintances made

_____
_____
_____
_____
_____
_____
_____
_____
_____
_____

Miscellaneous notes

_____
_____
_____
_____
_____
_____
_____
_____
_____
_____

RV PARK/CAMPGROUND: _____

DATE(S) VISITED: _____

SITE NUMBER: _____

OVERALL RATING ☆ ☆ ☆ ☆ ☆

BASIC CAMPSITE INFORMATION

- [ ] PULL-THROUGH
- [ ] BACK-IN
- [ ] SECLUDED SITE
- [ ] 50 AMP
- [ ] 30 AMP
- [ ] OPEN SITE
- [ ] WATER
- [ ] SEWER
- [ ] CONCRETE PAD

ADDITIONAL AMENITIES

- [ ] LAUNDRY
- [ ] WI-FI
- [ ] GAME RENTALS
- [ ] FIRE RING
- [ ] CABLE TV
- [ ] HIKING TRAILS
- [ ] SPORT ACTIVITY
- [ ] FITNESS ROOM
- [ ] FISHING
- [ ] POOL
- [ ] CLUBHOUSE
- [ ] BOATING
- [ ] RECEIVES MAIL
- [ ] SHOWERS
- [ ] ON-SITE STORE

NOISE LEVEL
- [ ] ACCEPTABLE
- [ ] UNACCEPTABLE

EXTRA FEES
- [ ] KIDS
- [ ] PETS

CLEANLINESS
- [ ] ACCEPTABLE
- [ ] UNACCEPTABLE

Surprising things we saw

Special events/outings

New acquaintances made

Miscellaneous notes

RV PARK/CAMPGROUND: _____
DATE(S) VISITED: _____
SITE NUMBER: _____
OVERALL RATING ☆ ☆ ☆ ☆ ☆

BASIC CAMPSITE INFORMATION

- [ ] PULL-THROUGH
- [ ] BACK-IN
- [ ] SECLUDED SITE
- [ ] 50 AMP
- [ ] 30 AMP
- [ ] OPEN SITE
- [ ] WATER
- [ ] SEWER
- [ ] CONCRETE PAD

ADDITIONAL AMENITIES

- [ ] LAUNDRY
- [ ] WI-FI
- [ ] GAME RENTALS
- [ ] FIRE RING
- [ ] CABLE TV
- [ ] HIKING TRAILS
- [ ] SPORT ACTIVITY
- [ ] FITNESS ROOM
- [ ] FISHING
- [ ] POOL
- [ ] CLUBHOUSE
- [ ] BOATING
- [ ] RECEIVES MAIL
- [ ] SHOWERS
- [ ] ON-SITE STORE

NOISE LEVEL
- [ ] ACCEPTABLE
- [ ] UNACCEPTABLE

EXTRA FEES
- [ ] KIDS
- [ ] PETS

CLEANLINESS
- [ ] ACCEPTABLE
- [ ] UNACCEPTABLE

Surprising things we saw

Special events/outings

New acquaintances made

Miscellaneous notes

RV PARK/CAMPGROUND: _____

DATE(S) VISITED: _____

SITE NUMBER: _____

OVERALL RATING ☆ ☆ ☆ ☆ ☆

BASIC CAMPSITE INFORMATION

- [ ] PULL-THROUGH
- [ ] BACK-IN
- [ ] SECLUDED SITE
- [ ] 50 AMP
- [ ] 30 AMP
- [ ] OPEN SITE
- [ ] WATER
- [ ] SEWER
- [ ] CONCRETE PAD

ADDITIONAL AMENITIES

- [ ] LAUNDRY
- [ ] WI-FI
- [ ] GAME RENTALS
- [ ] FIRE RING
- [ ] CABLE TV
- [ ] HIKING TRAILS
- [ ] SPORT ACTIVITY
- [ ] FITNESS ROOM
- [ ] FISHING
- [ ] POOL
- [ ] CLUBHOUSE
- [ ] BOATING
- [ ] RECEIVES MAIL
- [ ] SHOWERS
- [ ] ON-SITE STORE

NOISE LEVEL
- [ ] ACCEPTABLE
- [ ] UNACCEPTABLE

EXTRA FEES
- [ ] KIDS
- [ ] PETS

CLEANLINESS
- [ ] ACCEPTABLE
- [ ] UNACCEPTABLE

Surprising things we saw

Special events/outings

New acquaintances made

Miscellaneous notes

RV PARK/CAMPGROUND: _____
DATE(S) VISITED: _____
SITE NUMBER: _____
OVERALL RATING ☆ ☆ ☆ ☆ ☆

BASIC CAMPSITE INFORMATION

- [ ] PULL-THROUGH
- [ ] BACK-IN
- [ ] SECLUDED SITE
- [ ] 50 AMP
- [ ] 30 AMP
- [ ] OPEN SITE
- [ ] WATER
- [ ] SEWER
- [ ] CONCRETE PAD

ADDITIONAL AMENITIES

- [ ] LAUNDRY
- [ ] WI-FI
- [ ] GAME RENTALS
- [ ] FIRE RING
- [ ] CABLE TV
- [ ] HIKING TRAILS
- [ ] SPORT ACTIVITY
- [ ] FITNESS ROOM
- [ ] FISHING
- [ ] POOL
- [ ] CLUBHOUSE
- [ ] BOATING
- [ ] RECEIVES MAIL
- [ ] SHOWERS
- [ ] ON-SITE STORE

NOISE LEVEL
- [ ] ACCEPTABLE
- [ ] UNACCEPTABLE

EXTRA FEES
- [ ] KIDS
- [ ] PETS

CLEANLINESS
- [ ] ACCEPTABLE
- [ ] UNACCEPTABLE

Surprising things we saw

Special events/outings

New acquaintances made

Miscellaneous notes

RV PARK/CAMPGROUND: _____
DATE(S) VISITED: _____
SITE NUMBER: _____
OVERALL RATING ☆☆☆☆☆

BASIC CAMPSITE INFORMATION

- [ ] PULL-THROUGH
- [ ] BACK-IN
- [ ] SECLUDED SITE
- [ ] 50 AMP
- [ ] 30 AMP
- [ ] OPEN SITE
- [ ] WATER
- [ ] SEWER
- [ ] CONCRETE PAD

ADDITIONAL AMENITIES

- [ ] LAUNDRY
- [ ] WI-FI
- [ ] GAME RENTALS
- [ ] FIRE RING
- [ ] CABLE TV
- [ ] HIKING TRAILS
- [ ] SPORT ACTIVITY
- [ ] FITNESS ROOM
- [ ] FISHING
- [ ] POOL
- [ ] CLUBHOUSE
- [ ] BOATING
- [ ] RECEIVES MAIL
- [ ] SHOWERS
- [ ] ON-SITE STORE

NOISE LEVEL
- [ ] ACCEPTABLE
- [ ] UNACCEPTABLE

EXTRA FEES
- [ ] KIDS
- [ ] PETS

CLEANLINESS
- [ ] ACCEPTABLE
- [ ] UNACCEPTABLE

Surprising things we saw

Special events/outings

New acquaintances made

Miscellaneous notes

RV PARK/CAMPGROUND: _____
DATE(S) VISITED: _____
SITE NUMBER: _____
OVERALL RATING ☆☆☆☆☆

BASIC CAMPSITE INFORMATION

- [ ] PULL-THROUGH
- [ ] BACK-IN
- [ ] SECLUDED SITE
- [ ] 50 AMP
- [ ] 30 AMP
- [ ] OPEN SITE
- [ ] WATER
- [ ] SEWER
- [ ] CONCRETE PAD

ADDITIONAL AMENITIES

- [ ] LAUNDRY
- [ ] WI-FI
- [ ] GAME RENTALS
- [ ] FIRE RING
- [ ] CABLE TV
- [ ] HIKING TRAILS
- [ ] SPORT ACTIVITY
- [ ] FITNESS ROOM
- [ ] FISHING
- [ ] POOL
- [ ] CLUBHOUSE
- [ ] BOATING
- [ ] RECEIVES MAIL
- [ ] SHOWERS
- [ ] ON-SITE STORE

NOISE LEVEL
- [ ] ACCEPTABLE
- [ ] UNACCEPTABLE

EXTRA FEES
- [ ] KIDS
- [ ] PETS

CLEANLINESS
- [ ] ACCEPTABLE
- [ ] UNACCEPTABLE

Surprising things we saw

Special events/outings

New acquaintances made

Miscellaneous notes

RV PARK/CAMPGROUND: _____

DATE(S) VISITED: _____

SITE NUMBER: _____

OVERALL RATING ☆☆☆☆☆

BASIC CAMPSITE INFORMATION

- [ ] PULL-THROUGH
- [ ] BACK-IN
- [ ] SECLUDED SITE
- [ ] 50 AMP
- [ ] 30 AMP
- [ ] OPEN SITE
- [ ] WATER
- [ ] SEWER
- [ ] CONCRETE PAD

ADDITIONAL AMENITIES

- [ ] LAUNDRY
- [ ] WI-FI
- [ ] GAME RENTALS
- [ ] FIRE RING
- [ ] CABLE TV
- [ ] HIKING TRAILS
- [ ] SPORT ACTIVITY
- [ ] FITNESS ROOM
- [ ] FISHING
- [ ] POOL
- [ ] CLUBHOUSE
- [ ] BOATING
- [ ] RECEIVES MAIL
- [ ] SHOWERS
- [ ] ON-SITE STORE

NOISE LEVEL
- [ ] ACCEPTABLE
- [ ] UNACCEPTABLE

EXTRA FEES
- [ ] KIDS
- [ ] PETS

CLEANLINESS
- [ ] ACCEPTABLE
- [ ] UNACCEPTABLE

Surprising things we saw

_____
_____
_____
_____
_____
_____
_____
_____
_____

Special events/outings

_____
_____
_____
_____
_____
_____
_____
_____
_____

New acquaintances made

_____
_____
_____
_____
_____
_____
_____
_____
_____

Miscellaneous notes

_____
_____
_____
_____
_____
_____
_____
_____
_____

RV PARK/CAMPGROUND: _____

DATE(S) VISITED: _____

SITE NUMBER: _____

OVERALL RATING ☆ ☆ ☆ ☆ ☆

BASIC CAMPSITE INFORMATION

- [ ] PULL-THROUGH
- [ ] BACK-IN
- [ ] SECLUDED SITE
- [ ] 50 AMP
- [ ] 30 AMP
- [ ] OPEN SITE
- [ ] WATER
- [ ] SEWER
- [ ] CONCRETE PAD

ADDITIONAL AMENITIES

- [ ] LAUNDRY
- [ ] WI-FI
- [ ] GAME RENTALS
- [ ] FIRE RING
- [ ] CABLE TV
- [ ] HIKING TRAILS
- [ ] SPORT ACTIVITY
- [ ] FITNESS ROOM
- [ ] FISHING
- [ ] POOL
- [ ] CLUBHOUSE
- [ ] BOATING
- [ ] RECEIVES MAIL
- [ ] SHOWERS
- [ ] ON-SITE STORE

NOISE LEVEL
- [ ] ACCEPTABLE
- [ ] UNACCEPTABLE

EXTRA FEES
- [ ] KIDS
- [ ] PETS

CLEANLINESS
- [ ] ACCEPTABLE
- [ ] UNACCEPTABLE

Surprising things we saw

Special events/outings

New acquaintances made

Miscellaneous notes

RV PARK/CAMPGROUND: _____
DATE(S) VISITED: _____
SITE NUMBER: _____
OVERALL RATING ☆☆☆☆☆

BASIC CAMPSITE INFORMATION

- [ ] PULL-THROUGH
- [ ] BACK-IN
- [ ] SECLUDED SITE
- [ ] 50 AMP
- [ ] 30 AMP
- [ ] OPEN SITE
- [ ] WATER
- [ ] SEWER
- [ ] CONCRETE PAD

ADDITIONAL AMENITIES

- [ ] LAUNDRY
- [ ] WI-FI
- [ ] GAME RENTALS
- [ ] FIRE RING
- [ ] CABLE TV
- [ ] HIKING TRAILS
- [ ] SPORT ACTIVITY
- [ ] FITNESS ROOM
- [ ] FISHING
- [ ] POOL
- [ ] CLUBHOUSE
- [ ] BOATING
- [ ] RECEIVES MAIL
- [ ] SHOWERS
- [ ] ON-SITE STORE

NOISE LEVEL
- [ ] ACCEPTABLE
- [ ] UNACCEPTABLE

EXTRA FEES
- [ ] KIDS
- [ ] PETS

CLEANLINESS
- [ ] ACCEPTABLE
- [ ] UNACCEPTABLE

Surprising things we saw

Special events/outings

New acquaintances made

Miscellaneous notes

RV PARK/CAMPGROUND: _____

DATE(S) VISITED: _____

SITE NUMBER: _____

OVERALL RATING ☆ ☆ ☆ ☆ ☆

BASIC CAMPSITE INFORMATION

- [ ] PULL-THROUGH
- [ ] BACK-IN
- [ ] SECLUDED SITE
- [ ] 50 AMP
- [ ] 30 AMP
- [ ] OPEN SITE
- [ ] WATER
- [ ] SEWER
- [ ] CONCRETE PAD

ADDITIONAL AMENITIES

- [ ] LAUNDRY
- [ ] WI-FI
- [ ] GAME RENTALS
- [ ] FIRE RING
- [ ] CABLE TV
- [ ] HIKING TRAILS
- [ ] SPORT ACTIVITY
- [ ] FITNESS ROOM
- [ ] FISHING
- [ ] POOL
- [ ] CLUBHOUSE
- [ ] BOATING
- [ ] RECEIVES MAIL
- [ ] SHOWERS
- [ ] ON-SITE STORE

NOISE LEVEL
- [ ] ACCEPTABLE
- [ ] UNACCEPTABLE

EXTRA FEES
- [ ] KIDS
- [ ] PETS

CLEANLINESS
- [ ] ACCEPTABLE
- [ ] UNACCEPTABLE

Surprising things we saw

_____
_____
_____
_____
_____
_____
_____
_____
_____

Special events/outings

_____
_____
_____
_____
_____
_____
_____
_____
_____

New acquaintances made

_____
_____
_____
_____
_____
_____
_____
_____
_____

Miscellaneous notes

_____
_____
_____
_____
_____
_____
_____
_____
_____

RV PARK/CAMPGROUND: _____

DATE(S) VISITED: _____

SITE NUMBER: _____

OVERALL RATING ☆ ☆ ☆ ☆ ☆

BASIC CAMPSITE INFORMATION

- [ ] PULL-THROUGH
- [ ] BACK-IN
- [ ] SECLUDED SITE
- [ ] 50 AMP
- [ ] 30 AMP
- [ ] OPEN SITE
- [ ] WATER
- [ ] SEWER
- [ ] CONCRETE PAD

ADDITIONAL AMENITIES

- [ ] LAUNDRY
- [ ] WI-FI
- [ ] GAME RENTALS
- [ ] FIRE RING
- [ ] CABLE TV
- [ ] HIKING TRAILS
- [ ] SPORT ACTIVITY
- [ ] FITNESS ROOM
- [ ] FISHING
- [ ] POOL
- [ ] CLUBHOUSE
- [ ] BOATING
- [ ] RECEIVES MAIL
- [ ] SHOWERS
- [ ] ON-SITE STORE

NOISE LEVEL
- [ ] ACCEPTABLE
- [ ] UNACCEPTABLE

EXTRA FEES
- [ ] KIDS
- [ ] PETS

CLEANLINESS
- [ ] ACCEPTABLE
- [ ] UNACCEPTABLE

Surprising things we saw

Special events/outings

New acquaintances made

Miscellaneous notes

RV PARK/CAMPGROUND: _____
DATE(S) VISITED: _____
SITE NUMBER: _____
OVERALL RATING ☆ ☆ ☆ ☆ ☆

BASIC CAMPSITE INFORMATION

- [ ] PULL-THROUGH
- [ ] BACK-IN
- [ ] SECLUDED SITE
- [ ] 50 AMP
- [ ] 30 AMP
- [ ] OPEN SITE
- [ ] WATER
- [ ] SEWER
- [ ] CONCRETE PAD

ADDITIONAL AMENITIES

- [ ] LAUNDRY
- [ ] WI-FI
- [ ] GAME RENTALS
- [ ] FIRE RING
- [ ] CABLE TV
- [ ] HIKING TRAILS
- [ ] SPORT ACTIVITY
- [ ] FITNESS ROOM
- [ ] FISHING
- [ ] POOL
- [ ] CLUBHOUSE
- [ ] BOATING
- [ ] RECEIVES MAIL
- [ ] SHOWERS
- [ ] ON-SITE STORE

NOISE LEVEL
- [ ] ACCEPTABLE
- [ ] UNACCEPTABLE

EXTRA FEES
- [ ] KIDS
- [ ] PETS

CLEANLINESS
- [ ] ACCEPTABLE
- [ ] UNACCEPTABLE

Surprising Things We Saw

Special Events/Outings

New Acquaintances Made

Miscellaneous Notes

RV PARK/CAMPGROUND: _____
DATE(S) VISITED: _____
SITE NUMBER: _____
OVERALL RATING ☆ ☆ ☆ ☆ ☆

BASIC CAMPSITE INFORMATION

- ☐ PULL-THROUGH
- ☐ BACK-IN
- ☐ SECLUDED SITE
- ☐ 50 AMP
- ☐ 30 AMP
- ☐ OPEN SITE
- ☐ WATER
- ☐ SEWER
- ☐ CONCRETE PAD

ADDITIONAL AMENITIES

- ☐ LAUNDRY
- ☐ WI-FI
- ☐ GAME RENTALS
- ☐ FIRE RING
- ☐ CABLE TV
- ☐ HIKING TRAILS
- ☐ SPORT ACTIVITY
- ☐ FITNESS ROOM
- ☐ FISHING
- ☐ POOL
- ☐ CLUBHOUSE
- ☐ BOATING
- ☐ RECEIVES MAIL
- ☐ SHOWERS
- ☐ ON-SITE STORE

NOISE LEVEL
- ☐ ACCEPTABLE
- ☐ UNACCEPTABLE

EXTRA FEES
- ☐ KIDS
- ☐ PETS

CLEANLINESS
- ☐ ACCEPTABLE
- ☐ UNACCEPTABLE

Surprising Things We Saw

_____
_____
_____
_____
_____
_____
_____
_____
_____
_____

Special Events/Outings

_____
_____
_____
_____
_____
_____
_____
_____
_____
_____

New Acquaintances Made

_____
_____
_____
_____
_____
_____
_____
_____
_____
_____

Miscellaneous Notes

_____
_____
_____
_____
_____
_____
_____
_____
_____
_____

RV PARK/CAMPGROUND: _____
DATE(S) VISITED: _____
SITE NUMBER: _____
OVERALL RATING ☆☆☆☆☆

BASIC CAMPSITE INFORMATION

- ☐ PULL-THROUGH
- ☐ BACK-IN
- ☐ SECLUDED SITE
- ☐ 50 AMP
- ☐ 30 AMP
- ☐ OPEN SITE
- ☐ WATER
- ☐ SEWER
- ☐ CONCRETE PAD

ADDITIONAL AMENITIES

- ☐ LAUNDRY
- ☐ WI-FI
- ☐ GAME RENTALS
- ☐ FIRE RING
- ☐ CABLE TV
- ☐ HIKING TRAILS
- ☐ SPORT ACTIVITY
- ☐ FITNESS ROOM
- ☐ FISHING
- ☐ POOL
- ☐ CLUBHOUSE
- ☐ BOATING
- ☐ RECEIVES MAIL
- ☐ SHOWERS
- ☐ ON-SITE STORE

NOISE LEVEL
- ☐ ACCEPTABLE
- ☐ UNACCEPTABLE

EXTRA FEES
- ☐ KIDS
- ☐ PETS

CLEANLINESS
- ☐ ACCEPTABLE
- ☐ UNACCEPTABLE

Surprising things we saw

Special events/outings

New acquaintances made

Miscellaneous notes

RV PARK/CAMPGROUND: _____
DATE(S) VISITED: _____
SITE NUMBER: _____
OVERALL RATING ☆ ☆ ☆ ☆ ☆

BASIC CAMPSITE INFORMATION

- [ ] PULL-THROUGH
- [ ] BACK-IN
- [ ] SECLUDED SITE
- [ ] 50 AMP
- [ ] 30 AMP
- [ ] OPEN SITE
- [ ] WATER
- [ ] SEWER
- [ ] CONCRETE PAD

ADDITIONAL AMENITIES

- [ ] LAUNDRY
- [ ] WI-FI
- [ ] GAME RENTALS
- [ ] FIRE RING
- [ ] CABLE TV
- [ ] HIKING TRAILS
- [ ] SPORT ACTIVITY
- [ ] FITNESS ROOM
- [ ] FISHING
- [ ] POOL
- [ ] CLUBHOUSE
- [ ] BOATING
- [ ] RECEIVES MAIL
- [ ] SHOWERS
- [ ] ON-SITE STORE

NOISE LEVEL
- [ ] ACCEPTABLE
- [ ] UNACCEPTABLE

EXTRA FEES
- [ ] KIDS
- [ ] PETS

CLEANLINESS
- [ ] ACCEPTABLE
- [ ] UNACCEPTABLE

Surprising things we saw

Special events/outings

New acquaintances made

Miscellaneous notes

RV PARK/CAMPGROUND: _____

DATE(S) VISITED: _____

SITE NUMBER: _____

OVERALL RATING ☆ ☆ ☆ ☆ ☆

BASIC CAMPSITE INFORMATION

- [ ] PULL-THROUGH
- [ ] BACK-IN
- [ ] SECLUDED SITE
- [ ] 50 AMP
- [ ] 30 AMP
- [ ] OPEN SITE
- [ ] WATER
- [ ] SEWER
- [ ] CONCRETE PAD

ADDITIONAL AMENITIES

- [ ] LAUNDRY
- [ ] WI-FI
- [ ] GAME RENTALS
- [ ] FIRE RING
- [ ] CABLE TV
- [ ] HIKING TRAILS
- [ ] SPORT ACTIVITY
- [ ] FITNESS ROOM
- [ ] FISHING
- [ ] POOL
- [ ] CLUBHOUSE
- [ ] BOATING
- [ ] RECEIVES MAIL
- [ ] SHOWERS
- [ ] ON-SITE STORE

NOISE LEVEL
- [ ] ACCEPTABLE
- [ ] UNACCEPTABLE

EXTRA FEES
- [ ] KIDS
- [ ] PETS

CLEANLINESS
- [ ] ACCEPTABLE
- [ ] UNACCEPTABLE

Surprising things we saw

Special events/outings

New acquaintances made

Miscellaneous notes

RV PARK/CAMPGROUND: _____

DATE(S) VISITED: _____

SITE NUMBER: _____

OVERALL RATING ☆ ☆ ☆ ☆ ☆

BASIC CAMPSITE INFORMATION

- [ ] PULL-THROUGH
- [ ] BACK-IN
- [ ] SECLUDED SITE
- [ ] 50 AMP
- [ ] 30 AMP
- [ ] OPEN SITE
- [ ] WATER
- [ ] SEWER
- [ ] CONCRETE PAD

ADDITIONAL AMENITIES

- [ ] LAUNDRY
- [ ] WI-FI
- [ ] GAME RENTALS
- [ ] FIRE RING
- [ ] CABLE TV
- [ ] HIKING TRAILS
- [ ] SPORT ACTIVITY
- [ ] FITNESS ROOM
- [ ] FISHING
- [ ] POOL
- [ ] CLUBHOUSE
- [ ] BOATING
- [ ] RECEIVES MAIL
- [ ] SHOWERS
- [ ] ON-SITE STORE

NOISE LEVEL
- [ ] ACCEPTABLE
- [ ] UNACCEPTABLE

EXTRA FEES
- [ ] KIDS
- [ ] PETS

CLEANLINESS
- [ ] ACCEPTABLE
- [ ] UNACCEPTABLE

Surprising things we saw

Special events/outings

New acquaintances made

Miscellaneous notes

RV PARK/CAMPGROUND: _____
DATE(S) VISITED: _____
SITE NUMBER: _____
OVERALL RATING   ☆ ☆ ☆ ☆ ☆

BASIC CAMPSITE INFORMATION

- [ ] PULL-THROUGH
- [ ] BACK-IN
- [ ] SECLUDED SITE
- [ ] 50 AMP
- [ ] 30 AMP
- [ ] OPEN SITE
- [ ] WATER
- [ ] SEWER
- [ ] CONCRETE PAD

ADDITIONAL AMENITIES

- [ ] LAUNDRY
- [ ] WI-FI
- [ ] GAME RENTALS
- [ ] FIRE RING
- [ ] CABLE TV
- [ ] HIKING TRAILS
- [ ] SPORT ACTIVITY
- [ ] FITNESS ROOM
- [ ] FISHING
- [ ] POOL
- [ ] CLUBHOUSE
- [ ] BOATING
- [ ] RECEIVES MAIL
- [ ] SHOWERS
- [ ] ON-SITE STORE

NOISE LEVEL
- [ ] ACCEPTABLE
- [ ] UNACCEPTABLE

EXTRA FEES
- [ ] KIDS
- [ ] PETS

CLEANLINESS
- [ ] ACCEPTABLE
- [ ] UNACCEPTABLE

SURPRISING THINGS WE SAW	SPECIAL EVENTS/OUTINGS

NEW ACQUAINTANCES MADE	MISCELLANEOUS NOTES

RV PARK/CAMPGROUND: _____

DATE(S) VISITED: _____

SITE NUMBER: _____

OVERALL RATING ☆ ☆ ☆ ☆ ☆

BASIC CAMPSITE INFORMATION

- [ ] PULL-THROUGH
- [ ] BACK-IN
- [ ] SECLUDED SITE
- [ ] 50 AMP
- [ ] 30 AMP
- [ ] OPEN SITE
- [ ] WATER
- [ ] SEWER
- [ ] CONCRETE PAD

ADDITIONAL AMENITIES

- [ ] LAUNDRY
- [ ] WI-FI
- [ ] GAME RENTALS
- [ ] FIRE RING
- [ ] CABLE TV
- [ ] HIKING TRAILS
- [ ] SPORT ACTIVITY
- [ ] FITNESS ROOM
- [ ] FISHING
- [ ] POOL
- [ ] CLUBHOUSE
- [ ] BOATING
- [ ] RECEIVES MAIL
- [ ] SHOWERS
- [ ] ON-SITE STORE

NOISE LEVEL
- [ ] ACCEPTABLE
- [ ] UNACCEPTABLE

EXTRA FEES
- [ ] KIDS
- [ ] PETS

CLEANLINESS
- [ ] ACCEPTABLE
- [ ] UNACCEPTABLE

Surprising things we saw

Special events/outings

New acquaintances made

Miscellaneous notes

RV PARK/CAMPGROUND: _____
DATE(S) VISITED: _____
SITE NUMBER: _____
OVERALL RATING ☆ ☆ ☆ ☆ ☆

BASIC CAMPSITE INFORMATION

- [ ] PULL-THROUGH
- [ ] BACK-IN
- [ ] SECLUDED SITE
- [ ] 50 AMP
- [ ] 30 AMP
- [ ] OPEN SITE
- [ ] WATER
- [ ] SEWER
- [ ] CONCRETE PAD

ADDITIONAL AMENITIES

- [ ] LAUNDRY
- [ ] WI-FI
- [ ] GAME RENTALS
- [ ] FIRE RING
- [ ] CABLE TV
- [ ] HIKING TRAILS
- [ ] SPORT ACTIVITY
- [ ] FITNESS ROOM
- [ ] FISHING
- [ ] POOL
- [ ] CLUBHOUSE
- [ ] BOATING
- [ ] RECEIVES MAIL
- [ ] SHOWERS
- [ ] ON-SITE STORE

NOISE LEVEL
- [ ] ACCEPTABLE
- [ ] UNACCEPTABLE

EXTRA FEES
- [ ] KIDS
- [ ] PETS

CLEANLINESS
- [ ] ACCEPTABLE
- [ ] UNACCEPTABLE

| SURPRISING THINGS WE SAW | SPECIAL EVENTS/OUTINGS |

| NEW ACQUAINTANCES MADE | MISCELLANEOUS NOTES |

RV PARK/CAMPGROUND: _____

DATE(S) VISITED: _____

SITE NUMBER: _____

OVERALL RATING ☆ ☆ ☆ ☆ ☆

BASIC CAMPSITE INFORMATION

- [ ] PULL-THROUGH
- [ ] BACK-IN
- [ ] SECLUDED SITE
- [ ] 50 AMP
- [ ] 30 AMP
- [ ] OPEN SITE
- [ ] WATER
- [ ] SEWER
- [ ] CONCRETE PAD

ADDITIONAL AMENITIES

- [ ] LAUNDRY
- [ ] WI-FI
- [ ] GAME RENTALS
- [ ] FIRE RING
- [ ] CABLE TV
- [ ] HIKING TRAILS
- [ ] SPORT ACTIVITY
- [ ] FITNESS ROOM
- [ ] FISHING
- [ ] POOL
- [ ] CLUBHOUSE
- [ ] BOATING
- [ ] RECEIVES MAIL
- [ ] SHOWERS
- [ ] ON-SITE STORE

NOISE LEVEL
- [ ] ACCEPTABLE
- [ ] UNACCEPTABLE

EXTRA FEES
- [ ] KIDS
- [ ] PETS

CLEANLINESS
- [ ] ACCEPTABLE
- [ ] UNACCEPTABLE

Surprising things we saw

Special events/outings

New acquaintances made

Miscellaneous notes

RV PARK/CAMPGROUND: _____
DATE(S) VISITED: _____
SITE NUMBER: _____
OVERALL RATING ☆ ☆ ☆ ☆ ☆

BASIC CAMPSITE INFORMATION

- [ ] PULL-THROUGH
- [ ] BACK-IN
- [ ] SECLUDED SITE
- [ ] 50 AMP
- [ ] 30 AMP
- [ ] OPEN SITE
- [ ] WATER
- [ ] SEWER
- [ ] CONCRETE PAD

ADDITIONAL AMENITIES

- [ ] LAUNDRY
- [ ] WI-FI
- [ ] GAME RENTALS
- [ ] FIRE RING
- [ ] CABLE TV
- [ ] HIKING TRAILS
- [ ] SPORT ACTIVITY
- [ ] FITNESS ROOM
- [ ] FISHING
- [ ] POOL
- [ ] CLUBHOUSE
- [ ] BOATING
- [ ] RECEIVES MAIL
- [ ] SHOWERS
- [ ] ON-SITE STORE

NOISE LEVEL
- [ ] ACCEPTABLE
- [ ] UNACCEPTABLE

EXTRA FEES
- [ ] KIDS
- [ ] PETS

CLEANLINESS
- [ ] ACCEPTABLE
- [ ] UNACCEPTABLE

Surprising things we saw

_____
_____
_____
_____
_____
_____
_____
_____
_____

Special events/outings

_____
_____
_____
_____
_____
_____
_____
_____
_____

New acquaintances made

_____
_____
_____
_____
_____
_____
_____
_____
_____

Miscellaneous notes

_____
_____
_____
_____
_____
_____
_____
_____
_____

RV PARK/CAMPGROUND: _____
DATE(S) VISITED: _____
SITE NUMBER: _____
OVERALL RATING ☆ ☆ ☆ ☆ ☆

BASIC CAMPSITE INFORMATION

- [ ] PULL-THROUGH
- [ ] BACK-IN
- [ ] SECLUDED SITE
- [ ] 50 AMP
- [ ] 30 AMP
- [ ] OPEN SITE
- [ ] WATER
- [ ] SEWER
- [ ] CONCRETE PAD

ADDITIONAL AMENITIES

- [ ] LAUNDRY
- [ ] WI-FI
- [ ] GAME RENTALS
- [ ] FIRE RING
- [ ] CABLE TV
- [ ] HIKING TRAILS
- [ ] SPORT ACTIVITY
- [ ] FITNESS ROOM
- [ ] FISHING
- [ ] POOL
- [ ] CLUBHOUSE
- [ ] BOATING
- [ ] RECEIVES MAIL
- [ ] SHOWERS
- [ ] ON-SITE STORE

NOISE LEVEL

- [ ] ACCEPTABLE
- [ ] UNACCEPTABLE

EXTRA FEES

- [ ] KIDS
- [ ] PETS

CLEANLINESS

- [ ] ACCEPTABLE
- [ ] UNACCEPTABLE

Surprising things we saw

Special events/outings

New acquaintances made

Miscellaneous notes

RV PARK/CAMPGROUND: _____
DATE(S) VISITED: _____
SITE NUMBER: _____
OVERALL RATING ☆ ☆ ☆ ☆ ☆

BASIC CAMPSITE INFORMATION

- [ ] PULL-THROUGH
- [ ] BACK-IN
- [ ] SECLUDED SITE
- [ ] 50 AMP
- [ ] 30 AMP
- [ ] OPEN SITE
- [ ] WATER
- [ ] SEWER
- [ ] CONCRETE PAD

ADDITIONAL AMENITIES

- [ ] LAUNDRY
- [ ] WI-FI
- [ ] GAME RENTALS
- [ ] FIRE RING
- [ ] CABLE TV
- [ ] HIKING TRAILS
- [ ] SPORT ACTIVITY
- [ ] FITNESS ROOM
- [ ] FISHING
- [ ] POOL
- [ ] CLUBHOUSE
- [ ] BOATING
- [ ] RECEIVES MAIL
- [ ] SHOWERS
- [ ] ON-SITE STORE

NOISE LEVEL
- [ ] ACCEPTABLE
- [ ] UNACCEPTABLE

EXTRA FEES
- [ ] KIDS
- [ ] PETS

CLEANLINESS
- [ ] ACCEPTABLE
- [ ] UNACCEPTABLE

Surprising things we saw

Special events/outings

New acquaintances made

Miscellaneous notes

RV PARK/CAMPGROUND: _____
DATE(S) VISITED: _____
SITE NUMBER: _____
OVERALL RATING ☆☆☆☆☆

BASIC CAMPSITE INFORMATION

- [ ] PULL-THROUGH
- [ ] BACK-IN
- [ ] SECLUDED SITE
- [ ] 50 AMP
- [ ] 30 AMP
- [ ] OPEN SITE
- [ ] WATER
- [ ] SEWER
- [ ] CONCRETE PAD

ADDITIONAL AMENITIES

- [ ] LAUNDRY
- [ ] WI-FI
- [ ] GAME RENTALS
- [ ] FIRE RING
- [ ] CABLE TV
- [ ] HIKING TRAILS
- [ ] SPORT ACTIVITY
- [ ] FITNESS ROOM
- [ ] FISHING
- [ ] POOL
- [ ] CLUBHOUSE
- [ ] BOATING
- [ ] RECEIVES MAIL
- [ ] SHOWERS
- [ ] ON-SITE STORE

NOISE LEVEL
- [ ] ACCEPTABLE
- [ ] UNACCEPTABLE

EXTRA FEES
- [ ] KIDS
- [ ] PETS

CLEANLINESS
- [ ] ACCEPTABLE
- [ ] UNACCEPTABLE

Surprising things we saw

Special events/outings

New acquaintances made

Miscellaneous notes

RV PARK/CAMPGROUND: _____
DATE(S) VISITED: _____
SITE NUMBER: _____
OVERALL RATING ☆ ☆ ☆ ☆ ☆

BASIC CAMPSITE INFORMATION

- [ ] PULL-THROUGH
- [ ] BACK-IN
- [ ] SECLUDED SITE
- [ ] 50 AMP
- [ ] 30 AMP
- [ ] OPEN SITE
- [ ] WATER
- [ ] SEWER
- [ ] CONCRETE PAD

ADDITIONAL AMENITIES

- [ ] LAUNDRY
- [ ] WI-FI
- [ ] GAME RENTALS
- [ ] FIRE RING
- [ ] CABLE TV
- [ ] HIKING TRAILS
- [ ] SPORT ACTIVITY
- [ ] FITNESS ROOM
- [ ] FISHING
- [ ] POOL
- [ ] CLUBHOUSE
- [ ] BOATING
- [ ] RECEIVES MAIL
- [ ] SHOWERS
- [ ] ON-SITE STORE

NOISE LEVEL
- [ ] ACCEPTABLE
- [ ] UNACCEPTABLE

EXTRA FEES
- [ ] KIDS
- [ ] PETS

CLEANLINESS
- [ ] ACCEPTABLE
- [ ] UNACCEPTABLE

Surprising things we saw

_____
_____
_____
_____
_____
_____
_____
_____
_____

Special events/outings

_____
_____
_____
_____
_____
_____
_____
_____
_____

New acquaintances made

_____
_____
_____
_____
_____
_____
_____
_____
_____

Miscellaneous notes

_____
_____
_____
_____
_____
_____
_____
_____
_____

RV PARK/CAMPGROUND: _____

DATE(S) VISITED: _____

SITE NUMBER: _____

OVERALL RATING ☆ ☆ ☆ ☆ ☆

BASIC CAMPSITE INFORMATION

- [ ] PULL-THROUGH
- [ ] BACK-IN
- [ ] SECLUDED SITE
- [ ] 50 AMP
- [ ] 30 AMP
- [ ] OPEN SITE
- [ ] WATER
- [ ] SEWER
- [ ] CONCRETE PAD

ADDITIONAL AMENITIES

- [ ] LAUNDRY
- [ ] WI-FI
- [ ] GAME RENTALS
- [ ] FIRE RING
- [ ] CABLE TV
- [ ] HIKING TRAILS
- [ ] SPORT ACTIVITY
- [ ] FITNESS ROOM
- [ ] FISHING
- [ ] POOL
- [ ] CLUBHOUSE
- [ ] BOATING
- [ ] RECEIVES MAIL
- [ ] SHOWERS
- [ ] ON-SITE STORE

NOISE LEVEL
- [ ] ACCEPTABLE
- [ ] UNACCEPTABLE

EXTRA FEES
- [ ] KIDS
- [ ] PETS

CLEANLINESS
- [ ] ACCEPTABLE
- [ ] UNACCEPTABLE

Surprising things we saw

Special events/outings

New acquaintances made

Miscellaneous notes

RV PARK/CAMPGROUND: _____
DATE(S) VISITED: _____
SITE NUMBER: _____
OVERALL RATING ☆ ☆ ☆ ☆ ☆

BASIC CAMPSITE INFORMATION

- ☐ PULL-THROUGH
- ☐ BACK-IN
- ☐ SECLUDED SITE
- ☐ 50 AMP
- ☐ 30 AMP
- ☐ OPEN SITE
- ☐ WATER
- ☐ SEWER
- ☐ CONCRETE PAD

ADDITIONAL AMENITIES

- ☐ LAUNDRY
- ☐ WI-FI
- ☐ GAME RENTALS
- ☐ FIRE RING
- ☐ CABLE TV
- ☐ HIKING TRAILS
- ☐ SPORT ACTIVITY
- ☐ FITNESS ROOM
- ☐ FISHING
- ☐ POOL
- ☐ CLUBHOUSE
- ☐ BOATING
- ☐ RECEIVES MAIL
- ☐ SHOWERS
- ☐ ON-SITE STORE

NOISE LEVEL
- ☐ ACCEPTABLE
- ☐ UNACCEPTABLE

EXTRA FEES
- ☐ KIDS
- ☐ PETS

CLEANLINESS
- ☐ ACCEPTABLE
- ☐ UNACCEPTABLE

Surprising things we saw

_____
_____
_____
_____
_____
_____
_____
_____
_____

Special events/outings

_____
_____
_____
_____
_____
_____
_____
_____
_____

New acquaintances made

_____
_____
_____
_____
_____
_____
_____
_____
_____

Miscellaneous notes

_____
_____
_____
_____
_____
_____
_____
_____
_____

RV PARK/CAMPGROUND: _____
DATE(S) VISITED: _____
SITE NUMBER: _____
OVERALL RATING ☆ ☆ ☆ ☆ ☆

BASIC CAMPSITE INFORMATION

- [ ] PULL-THROUGH
- [ ] BACK-IN
- [ ] SECLUDED SITE
- [ ] 50 AMP
- [ ] 30 AMP
- [ ] OPEN SITE
- [ ] WATER
- [ ] SEWER
- [ ] CONCRETE PAD

ADDITIONAL AMENITIES

- [ ] LAUNDRY
- [ ] WI-FI
- [ ] GAME RENTALS
- [ ] FIRE RING
- [ ] CABLE TV
- [ ] HIKING TRAILS
- [ ] SPORT ACTIVITY
- [ ] FITNESS ROOM
- [ ] FISHING
- [ ] POOL
- [ ] CLUBHOUSE
- [ ] BOATING
- [ ] RECEIVES MAIL
- [ ] SHOWERS
- [ ] ON-SITE STORE

NOISE LEVEL
- [ ] ACCEPTABLE
- [ ] UNACCEPTABLE

EXTRA FEES
- [ ] KIDS
- [ ] PETS

CLEANLINESS
- [ ] ACCEPTABLE
- [ ] UNACCEPTABLE

Surprising things we saw

Special events/outings

New acquaintances made

Miscellaneous notes

From the author…

Thanks so much for using this book! I trust it was a help and inspiration to you, providing a great snapshot of your adventurous heart.

Would you mind taking a minute to review my book on Amazon?

I certainly appreciate it!

Made in the USA
Monee, IL
20 December 2020